Contents

Cells 1
- Eukaryotes and prokaryotes
- Cell components
- Cell specialisation

Stem cells, microscopy, and microorganisms. 2
- Cell differentiation
- Human stem cells
- Plant stem cells
- Microscopy
- Culturing microorganisms

Transport in cells 3
- Surface area to volume ratio
- Diffusion
- Osmosis
- Active transport

Transport systems 4
- Cells, tissues, and organs
- The digestive system
- Lung anatomy
- Heart anatomy
- The circulatory system

Blood and heart disease 5
- Blood vessels
- Components of blood
- Coronary heart disease and heart problems
- Lifestyle factors and risk of disease

Human health and enzymes 6
- Physical and mental health
- Cancer
- Digestive enzymes
- Lock and key theory
- Denaturing enzymes

Plant transport systems 7
- Plant tissues
- Xylem and phloem
- Transpiration and translocation
- Root hair cells

Pathogens and non-specific immunity 8
- Pathogens
- Non-specific immunity
- Viral diseases
- Bacterial, fungal, and protist diseases

The immune system and drugs 9
- The immune system
- Vaccination
- Antibiotics
- Modern and historical drug development

Plant disease and monoclonal antibodies 10
- Plant defences
- Plant diseases
- Producing and using monoclonal antibodies

Photosynthesis and respiration 11
- Photosynthesis
- Rate of photosynthesis
- Aerobic respiration
- Anaerobic respiration
- Metabolism and response to exercise
- Lactic acid accumulation

The nervous system and homeostasis. 12
- The nervous system
- Synapses
- Reflex arcs
- Nerves and neurones
- Homeostasis

The brain and the eye 13
- The brain
- Studying the brain
- The eye
- Accommodation and adaptation to dim light
- Myopia and hyperopia

Hormone regulation and waste excretion. 14
- The endocrine system
- Thermoregulation
- Control of blood glucose and diabetes
- Adrenaline and thyroxine
- Water balance and protein removal
- The kidney

Contents

Reproductive hormones and plant hormones 15
    Hormones in reproduction and the menstrual cycle
    Contraception
    Infertility
    Tropisms
    Uses of plant hormones

Cell division, reproduction, and DNA structure 16
    Mitosis and meiosis
    Sexual and asexual reproduction
    DNA
    DNA structure
    Gene expression and mutations
    The Human Genome Project

DNA synthesis and inheritance 17
    Transcription
    Translation
    Inheritance terminology
    Punnett squares and family trees
    Determining sex
    Inherited disorders

Genetic engineering and modification 18
    Selective breeding
    Genetic engineering
    Genetically modified (GM) organisms
    Genetically modified animals and bacteria
    Cloning

Evolution and natural selection 10
    Variation
    Evolution
    Theory of evolution by natural selection
    Evidence for evolution
    Mendelian genetics
    Solving antibiotic resistance

Species and classification 20
    Speciation
    Adaptations
    Classification and Linnaeus
    Updates to classification
    Extinction

Ecosystems 21
    Competition
    Interdependence
    Sampling
    Biotic and abiotic factors
    Predation

Resource cycles and environmental change 22
    The carbon cycle
    The water cycle
    Effects of environmental change
    Global warming

Biodiversity and environmental management 23
    Biodiversity
    Land use
    Deforestation
    Waste management
    Decomposition

Biomass and trophic levels 24
    Pyramids of biomass
    Transfer of biomass
    Food chains and trophic levels

Food supply and biotechnology 25
    Factors affecting food security
    Farming techniques
    Sustainable fisheries
    Biotechnology

Science skills: Experimental procedures 26
    Scientific processes
    Apparatus and equipment
    Variables
    Safe experiments

Science skills: Presenting and using data 27
    Presenting data
    Rounding and standard form
    Equations
    Interpreting graphs

Science skills: Measuring results 28
    Accuracy and precision
    Uncertainty, errors, and anomalies
    Mean and range
    Units and prefixes

Cells

Eukaryotes and prokaryotes

Eukaryotic cells	Prokaryotic cells
Plant and animal cells	Bacterial cells
Cell membrane	Cell membrane surrounded by a cell wall
Cytoplasm	Cytoplasm
Genetic material enclosed in a nucleus	Genetic material is a single DNA loop and sometimes small rings of DNA called plasmids, not enclosed in a nucleus.
Larger (5 μm – 100 μm)	Smaller (1 μm – 10 μm)

Cell components

- Animal and plant cells share some, but not all organelles.
- **Mitochondria** are the site of aerobic respiration where energy is released from glucose.
- **Cytoplasm** is water-based and contains lots of the organelles. It is where most cell reactions take place.
- Nucleus contains **deoxyribonucleic acid (DNA)**, which is the genetic information that controls the cell. DNA is organised into chromosomes.
- **Cell membrane** encloses the cell and controls which substances go in and out. Many simple substances travel by diffusion.
- **Ribosomes** are the site of protein synthesis.
- **Chloroplasts** (plant cells) contain the green pigment chlorophyll, which absorbs light for photosynthesis.
- **Cell wall** (plant and algal cells) made of cellulose, which strengthens the cell.

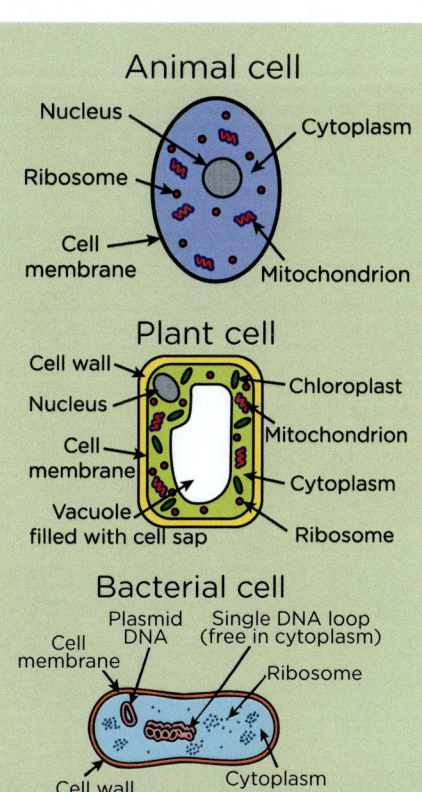

Cell specialisation

Cell	Function	Specialised structure
Sperm cell (animal)	Travel through the female reproductive system to fertilise an ovum (egg cell)	• Tail to swim • Large number of mitochondria to release energy to swim
Nerve cell (animal)	Transmit electrical signals quickly through nervous system	• Long cell extension (axons) • Myelin sheath insulator increases the speed of transmission of electrical impulses • Cell body has extensions to pick up signals from neighbouring cells
Muscle cell (animal)	Contract and relax	• Large number of mitochondria to provide energy for contraction
Root hair cell (plant)	Absorb water and minerals from soil	• Small thin extension to increase surface area for absorption of water and minerals
Xylem (plant)	Carry water and dissolved minerals upwards from roots up plant stems for transpiration	• Empty dead cells form long hollow tubes with no end walls • Lignin inside walls supports plant weight
Phloem cell (plant)	Carry sucrose in cell sap from leaves to other parts of the plant via translocation	• Living cells form tubes • Contain few organelles so sugar travels easily • End walls contain small holes (sieve plates)

Stem cells, microscopy, and microorganisms

Cell differentiation
- Cell differentiation is the **specialisation** of cells by acquiring **different sub-cellular structures**. This is required so cells can perform their specific functions.
- Cells differentiate to form different types of cells:
  - Most animal cells differentiate at an early stage. In mature animals, cell division is restricted to repairing and replacing damaged and old cells.
  - Many plant cells can differentiate throughout life.

Human stem cells
- A stem cell is an **undifferentiated** cell capable of replication and differentiation into other types of cell.
- In human embryos, **embryonic stem cells** can differentiate into any type of specialised human cell (totipotent). Once it has differentiated, it cannot change back or switch cell type.
- In adult bone marrow, **adult stem cells** can form many specific cell types, such as blood stem cells producing blood cells (multipotent).
- Human stem cells can be used in **therapeutic cloning** to help conditions such as diabetes and paralysis.
  - An embryo is produced with the same genes as the patient.
  - Stem cells from the embryo are not rejected by the patient's body.
  - Potential risks include transfer of viral infection and some people have ethical or religious objections.

Plant stem cells
All specs except: CIE, Pearson IGCSE
- In plant **meristem tissue**, stem cells can differentiate into any type of plant cell throughout the life of the plant.
- Plant stem cells are used to artificially produce clones of plants as this process is quick and economically efficient.
- Rare species can be cloned to prevent extinction, and crops with features such as disease resistance are cloned to make large numbers of identical plants for farmers.

Microscopy
- **Light microscopes** were invented first, with a maximum resolution of 200nm.
  - The eyepiece lens often has x10 magnification, then the 3 objective lenses will have different magnifications (x5, x10, and x25).
  - The stage holds the specimen which is on a microscope slide under a cover slip.
  - Course focus moves the stage closer and further from the chosen objective lens to roughly focus the sample, and fine focus moves the stage slowly to adjust.
- **Electron microscopes** were invented later and have a max. resolution of 0.1 nm, allowing for a better understanding of sub-cellular structures.
  - **Transmission electron microscope (TEM)** fires a beam of electrons through a thin slice of the specimen. Electrons that pass through the specimen are detected and used to make the image.
  - **Scanning electron microscope (SEM)** fires a beam of electrons across the surface of the specimen. Electrons scatter from the surface and are detected to make the image.

Culturing microorganisms
All specs except: CIE, Pearson IGCSE
- Bacteria multiply by cell division **(binary fission)** as frequently as once every 20 minutes, but only if they have enough nutrients and a suitable temperature.
  - Bacteria can be grown in a nutrient broth solution.
  - Bacteria can be grown as colonies on an agar gel plate.
- Uncontaminated cultures of microorganisms are used to investigate the action of **disinfectants** and **antibiotics**. They are prepared using **aseptic technique:**
  - Petri dishes and culture media must be sterilised before use to prevent growing foreign microorganisms.
  - Inoculating loops must be sterilised by passing them through a flame before being used to transfer microorganisms to the petri dish.
  - The Petri dish should be stored upside down with the lid secured with adhesive tape to reduce the contamination risk from airborne microorganisms and stop condensation from pooling.
  - Cultures should be incubated at 25 °C to encourage growth of the microorganisms without growing contaminating microorganisms from humans (which grow best at 37 °C).

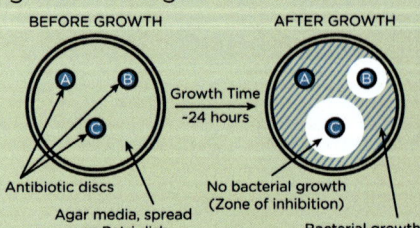

Effect of three antibiotics (A, B and C) on bacterial growth:
- A = No effect
- B = Inhibits growth weakly
- C = Inhibits growth strongly

Transport in cells

Surface area to volume ratio
- A large surface area to volume ratio increases the rate of diffusion.
- To calculate surface area to volume ratio, divide the surface area by the volume.
- **Single-celled organisms** have a large surface area to volume ratio so molecules can move into and out of the cell to meet the needs of the organism.
- **Multicellular organisms** have a small surface area to volume ratio so require an exchange surface and transport system to move substances around the organism.

Diffusion
- Diffusion is the net movement of particles in solution or of a gas from an area of **higher concentration to an area of lower concentration.** Examples include oxygen and carbon dioxide in gas exchange, and waste urea from cells into the blood plasma for excretion in the kidney.
- **Factors affecting diffusion rate:**
  - Steeper concentration gradients increase diffusion rate.
  - Higher temperatures increase diffusion rate
  - Increasing surface area increases diffusion rate.
- The effectiveness of **diffusion exchange surface in humans** is increased by having:
  - A large surface area
  - A thin membrane (short distance for diffusion)
  - Efficient blood supply in animals
  - Well-ventilated in animals for gas exchange
  - Moist membrane in animals for gas exchange

Osmosis
- Osmosis is the diffusion of water from a dilute solution to a concentrated solution through a partially permeable membrane, such as the cell membrane.
- Cells can be placed in solutions with different relative concentrations.
  - **Isotonic:** concentration inside the cell is the same as the concentration of the solution. No net movement of water.
  - **Hypertonic:** concentration of the solution is higher than the concentration inside the cell.
  - **Hypotonic:** concentration of the solution is lower than the concentration inside the cell.
- The water uptake rate in grams/hour is equal to the change in mass divided by the time in minutes.

Solution	Animal cell	Plant cell
Hypertonic (e.g. salty brine)	Shrunken/shrivelled	Flaccid → plasmolysed
Hypotonic (e.g. pure water)	Swell and burst	Turgid

Active transport
- Active transport is the movement of substances from a more dilute solution to a more concentrated solution.
- As this movement is against a concentration gradient, it requires energy from respiration.
- Active transport facilitates:
  - The absorption of mineral ions from very dilute solutions in the soil into plant root hairs. Plants require ions for healthy growth.
  - The absorption of sugar molecules from lower concentrations in the gut into the blood, which has a higher sugar concentration. Sugar molecules are needed for cell respiration.

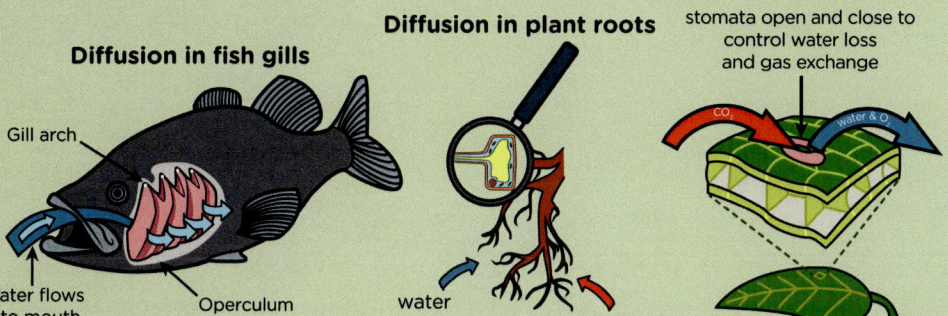

Transport systems

Cells, tissues, and organs

- Cells are the basic building blocks of all living organisms.
- Tissues are groups of cells with a similar structure and function.
- Organs are groups of tissues performing specific functions.
- An organ system is made up of organs.
- Organ systems work together to form organisms.

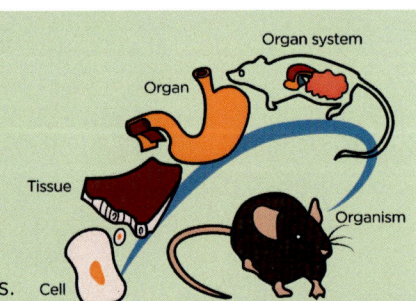

The digestive system

All specs except: Edexcel

- The digestive system is an organ system.
- Digestion is the breakdown of large, insoluble food into small, soluble molecules, which are absorbed into the bloodstream.
- The products of digestion are used to build new carbohydrates, lipids and proteins. Some glucose is used in respiration.

Structures of the digestive system:
- **Mouth:** ingests food; teeth break food into smaller pieces to increase surface area for digestive enzyme action.
- **Salivary glands:** produce slightly alkaline saliva containing enzymes that break down starch.
- **Oesophagus:** peristalsis (contraction and relaxation of circular and longitudinal muscles) moves food into the stomach.
- **Stomach:** churns food with hydrochloric acid, killing microorganisms. Stomach acids break down proteins.
- **Small intestine:** contains enzymes to break down food and villi to absorb products of digestion (e.g. glucose and amino acids absorbed into the capillaries/bloodstream, fatty acids and glycerol absorbed into the lymph (lacteal).
- **Large intestine:** absorbs remaining water, forming faeces.
- **Rectum and anus:** stores and egests faeces.
- **Liver:** produces bile.
- **Gall bladder:** stores bile.
- **Pancreas:** produces digestive enzymes.

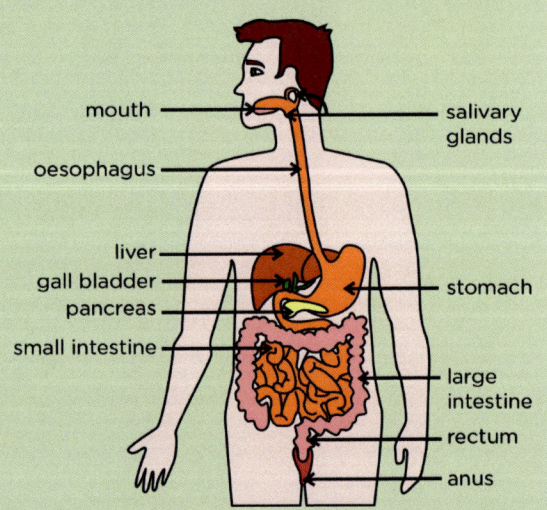

Lung anatomy

All specs except: Edexcel, OCR A, OCR B

- Carbon dioxide is removed from the blood in the lungs to prevent the pH of the blood becoming too acidic.
- Lungs are adapted for gas exchange:
  ○ Alveoli have a thin wall only one cell thick so there is a short distance for diffusion.
  ○ Moist membrane accelerates the diffusion of gases.
  ○ Shape of alveoli provides large surface area for diffusion.
  ○ Extensive capillary network surrounding alveoli.
  ○ Well-ventilated to maintain a large diffusion gradient.

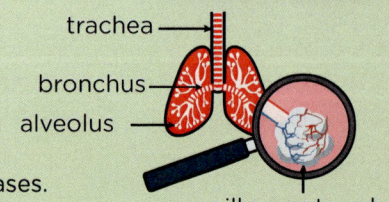

Heart anatomy

- Valves prevent the backflow of blood.
- The heart muscle cells are supplied by the coronary arteries, delivering oxygen for aerobic respiration to provide energy for the heart to contract.
- The resting heart rate is controlled by a group of pacemaker cells located in the wall of the right atrium.
- Irregularities in the heart rate are corrected using artificial pacemakers.

The circulatory system

- The heart is an organ that pumps blood around the body in a **double circulatory system** (blood passes through the heart twice in one complete circuit of the body):
  ○ The **right ventricle** pumps deoxygenated blood to the lungs for gas exchange. Oxygen enters the blood and waste carbon dioxide leaves the blood.
  ○ The **left ventricle** pumps oxygenated blood around the rest of the body where body cells use the oxygen for aerobic respiration to provide energy.
  ○ Respiration also produces waste carbon dioxide, which is transported in the blood and exhaled via the lungs.
- **Heart rate:** number of times a heart beats per minute.
- **Stroke volume:** amount of blood ejected from the heart per heartbeat.
- **Cardiac output:** volume of blood being pumped by the heart per minute (i.e. heart rate × stroke volume).

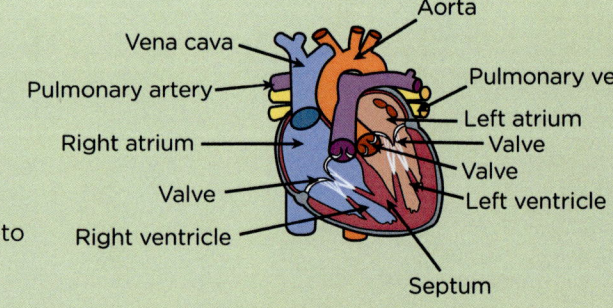

Blood and heart disease

Blood vessels

- **Arteries:** transport oxygenated blood away from the heart at a high pressure so it can reach the rest of the body (apart from the pulmonary artery which carries deoxygenated blood). They have a thick outer protective wall, and a thick muscle and elastic layer that can stretch to withstand high-pressure blood flow. There is a small lumen to maintain high pressure and smooth lining to minimise friction.
- **Veins:** transport deoxygenated blood back to the heart at a low pressure (apart from the pulmonary vein that carries oxygenated blood from the lungs). Veins have a thinner walls and muscle layers than arteries as blood pressure is lower. They have a large lumen and smooth lining to minimise friction, and valves to ensure blood only flows one way.
- **Capillaries:** surround respiring cells and transport blood at a very low pressure so it moves slowly to allow time for gas exchange with neighbouring cells. Blood plasma passes through capillary walls into tissues where it is called tissue fluid. Capillaries have a very small lumen so blood is in contact with capillary wall to create a short distance of diffusion for gases. Their walls are one cell thick so there is a very short distance of diffusion.

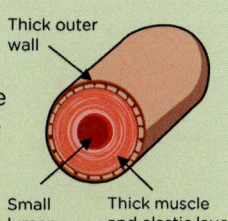
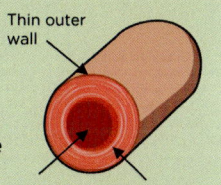
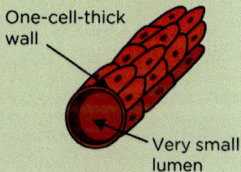

Components of blood

- **Red blood cells:** transports oxygen around the body.
  - Contains haemoglobin, which binds to oxygen.
  - Biconcave shape gives a high surface area to volume ratio.
  - No nucleus to maximise space for more haemoglobin.
- **White blood cells:** destroy pathogens as part of immune system.
  - **Phagocytes** engulf pathogens and digest them using enzymes. Phagocytes have a lobed nucleus and a granulated cytoplasm (granules contain enzymes).
  - **Lymphocytes** produce antibodies to clump pathogens together. Lymphocytes are smaller, have a large nucleus and no granules.
- **Platelets:** when the skin is wounded, they release clotting factors, which turn fibrinogen in the plasma into fibrin, forming a mesh that sticks platelets together to form a scab.
- **Plasma:** other blood components are suspended in plasma, and it transports glucose, amino acids, carbon dioxide and urea. Plasma is straw-coloured aqueous liquid mostly made up of water which dissolves nutrients.

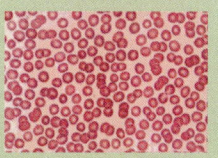
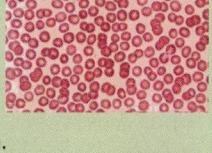

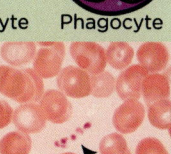

Coronary heart disease and heart problems

All specs except: OCR A, CIE

- Coronary heart disease can lead to a **heart attack** which is when fatty material (plaque) builds up in the coronary arteries, narrowing them and reducing the flexibility of the artery lining, which reduces blood flow (atherosclerosis). This means less oxygen is delivered to the heart muscle, so heart muscle cells die.
- **Treatments for coronary heart disease** include **stents** (to keep the coronary arteries open), **statins** (to reduce blood cholesterol levels to slow down the rate of fatty material deposit) and **heart transplants**. Artificial hearts are sometimes used to keep patients alive whilst waiting for a transplant or to help during recovery.
- **Faulty heart valves:** prevent the valve from opening fully, and can leak. Blood flows backwards, reducing the efficiency at which blood flows around the body, meaning cells do not receive as much glucose and oxygen for respiration. Treatments for faulty heart valves include replacement biological valves from donors, or replacement artificial mechanical valves.
- Other heart problems include breathlessness, tiredness, dizziness, and chest pain.

Treatment	Advantages	Disadvantages
Drugs	• Cheap • Can reduce cholesterol or reduce clotting	• Not suitable if you have liver disease • Side effects • Must be taken for life • Anti-clotting drugs increase bleed risk
Mechanical	• Less dangerous than transplants • Fast recovery	• Biological valves may need to be replaced • Mechanical valves may cause blood clots
Transplant	• Lifesaving • Life can return to normal	• Slow recovery and risk of immune rejection • Expensive operation • Patient must take immunosuppressants for life • Few donor hearts available

Lifestyle factors and risk of disease

All specs except: CIE, Pearson IGCSE

- **Lifestyle factors** can increase the risk of cardiovascular disease, such as poor diet (high in fat and cholesterol), smoking, alcohol, or lack of exercise.
- **Pre-existing conditions** can increase the risk of cardiovascular disease, including type 2 diabetes (of which obesity is a risk factor), high blood pressure, or high cholesterol
- Many diseases are caused by the interaction of **multiple risk factors.**
- Risk factors are linked to an increased rate of a disease, but a causal mechanism has not been proven for all of them. For instance, **carcinogens** are substances in the body or environment (e.g. ionising radiation) that are linked to causing cancer.
- Non-communicable diseases are more common in poorer areas as inhabitants may be more exposed to negative risk factors, such as lack of fresh food, water, and shelter, and may be more exposed to substances such as pollutants.
- Non-communicable diseases have costs at local, national, and global levels, decreasing quality of life and life expectancy, and putting emotional and financial strains on friends/family if a patient is unable to work or engage in daily life.

Human health and enzymes

Physical and mental health
- Health is a state of physical and mental well-being.
- Causes of ill health include **communicable disease** (can pass from one organism to another), **non-communicable disease** (cannot pass from one organism to another), diet, stress, and life circumstances.
- Different types of disease may interact. For instance, defects in the immune system may mean an individual is more likely to suffer from infectious diseases, and immune reactions caused by a pathogen can trigger allergies, such as skin rashes and asthma.
- Severe physical ill health can lead to mental illnesses, such as depression.

Cancer
All specs except: CIE, Pearson IGCSE
- Cancer is the result of **uncontrolled growth and division in cells.**
- **Benign tumours** are not cancers; they are growths of abnormal cells that are contained in one area, usually within a membrane, but do not invade other parts of the body.
- **Malignant tumours** are cancers: they invade neighbouring tissues and spread to different parts of the body in the blood where they form secondary tumours (by metastasis).
- Signs of cancer include tumorous lumps, a long-term cough and unexplained bleeding or weight loss
- Different cancers have different risk factors, but common factors include smoking and alcohol, obesity, age, infections (e.g. hepatitis, HPV), ionising radiation (e.g. UV from the sun), environmental pollutants from industry, and genetic disorders.
- Cancer can be screened (e.g. blood tests and X-ray images).
- Cancer may be treated with chemotherapy and radiotherapy; however, this can kill healthy cells too, with side effects including sickness and hair loss.

Digestive enzymes
- Saliva produced by salivary glands contains the carbohydrase enzymes amylase and maltase, which catalyses the breakdown of carbohydrates to simple sugars.
  - **Amylase:** turns starch into maltose.
  - **Maltase:** turns maltose into glucose.
- **Proteases** produced in the stomach begin the digestion of proteins into amino acids.
- **Lipases** break down lipids (fats and oils) into fatty acids and glycerol.
- The pancreas produces **carbohydrase**, protease and lipase enzymes and releases them into the small intestine.
- The liver produces **bile**, which is stored in the gall bladder.
- Bile neutralises the acid entering the small intestine from the stomach and emulsifies fats (breaks them up into small droplets, increasing the surface area for lipase action).

Lock and key theory
- Enzymes catalyse (speed up) specific reactions in organisms due to the shape of their active site.
- The substrate is the reactants of the reaction to be catalysed.
- The 'lock and key theory' proposes that the shape of the substrate is complementary to the active site so can bind to it, which allows the enzyme to break the bonds holding the substrate together.
- Enzyme-catalysed reactions contribute to metabolism.

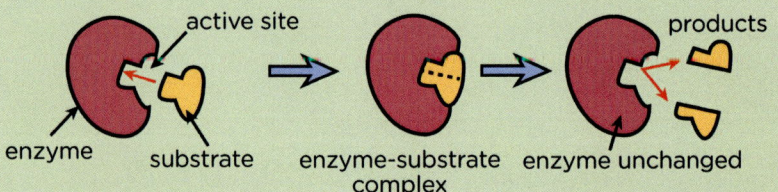

Denaturing enzymes
- Enzymes work at optimum conditions, and any movement away from these conditions lowers the enzyme activity and effectiveness.

Body part	Enzyme	Optimum pH	Optimum temp.
Mouth	Amylase, maltase	Alkaline	37 °C
Stomach	Protease	Acidic	37 °C
Small intestine	Lipase, protease, amylase, maltase	Alkaline	37 °C

- Enzymes are denatured by extremes of pH and temperature as the shape of the active site permanently changes so the substrate no longer fits.
- As temperature increases, enzymes and their substrate have more kinetic energy, so they will more frequently collide and enzyme activity increases.
- If temperature increases above the optimum temperature for an enzyme, it will denature because the bonds holding it together will break.

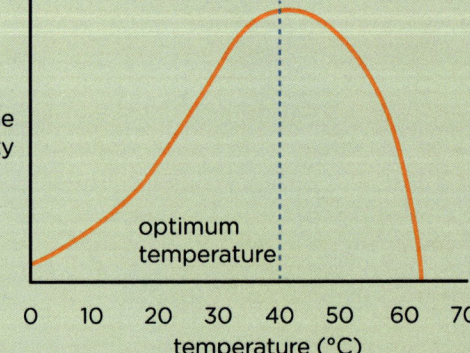

Plant transport systems

Plant tissues

- The roots, stem and leaves form a plant organ system for transport of substances around the plant.
- The leaf is a plant organ made up of numerous plant tissues.

Tissue	Function	Structure
Epidermal tissues	Protects against water loss, regulates gas exchange in leaves, and regulates water and mineral uptake in roots	• Outermost layer one cell thick and transparent so light passes through • Contains stomata and guard cells on bottom of leaf
Palisade mesophyll	Major site of photosynthesis	• Found towards upper surface of leaf so lots of light reaches it • Tightly-packed cells containing lots of chloroplast to maximise photosynthesis
Spongy mesophyll	Gas exchange	• Found towards bottom of leaves close to where gas enters through stomata • Space between cells for gas diffusion • Large surface area in contact with air spaces to maximise gas exchange
Meristem tissue	Stem cells are produced for plant growth	• Found at the growing tips of shoots and roots

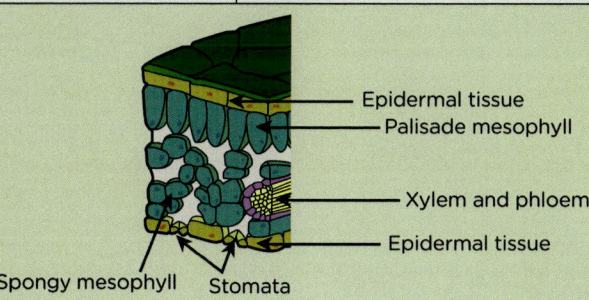

Xylem and phloem

- Xylem and phloem are found together in the vascular bundle.
- Xylem tissue transports water and mineral ions up from the roots to the leaves via the stem. It is made of hollow tubes without end walls, strengthened by lignin.
- Phloem tissue transports dissolved sucrose from the leaves (made from glucose from photosynthesis) to the rest of the plant for use or storage. This is called translocation.
- Cell sap in phloem tissue can move from one cell to the next through pores in the end walls.

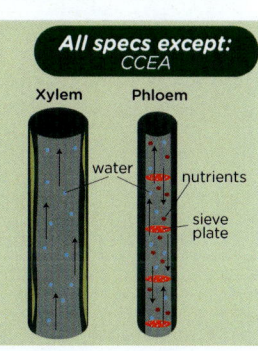

Transpiration and translocation

- The movement of water through a plant occurs through transpiration, where water is pulled through the plant as it is continuously released from the leaves through **stomata**.
  - Water enters the root hair cells by osmosis and travels through them to the xylem.
  - Water travels up the xylem in the stem into the spongy mesophyll of the leaf by osmosis.
  - Water evaporates out of spongy mesophyll cells, forming water vapour in the air spaces of the spongy mesophyll.
  - Water vapour diffuses out of the leaf through stomata.
- Stomata control gas exchange and water loss by opening and closing, which is controlled by guard cells.
  - When guard cells are turgid, the stomata are open, allowing water vapour to leave the leaf and carbon dioxide to enter for photosynthesis.
  - When dehydrated, guard cells are flaccid and the stomata are closed, preventing further water loss.
- Transpiration rate equal to the decrease in mass or volume of water absorbed divided by time. This rate is affected by various factors:

Factor	Effect on transpiration rate
Temperature	Transpiration rate increases as temperature increases because molecules have greater kinetic energy, speeding up the rate of evaporation and diffusion.
Humidity	Transpiration rate decreases as humidity increases as the atmosphere has a higher concentration of water vapour, decreasing the diffusion of water vapour out of the leaf.
Air movement	Transpiration rate increases as wind increases as it carries water vapour from the leaf.
Light intensity	Transpiration rate increases as light intensity increases as the stomata open wider to allow carbon dioxide in for photosynthesis, allowing water vapour to escape.

Root hair cells

- Root hair cells are adapted for the efficient uptake of water by osmosis and mineral ions by active transport:
  - Thin: short distance for osmosis and active transport
  - Long: penetrate between soil particles to come into contact with water and mineral ions
  - Large surface area: maximise osmosis and active transport
  - Lots of mitochondria for active transport

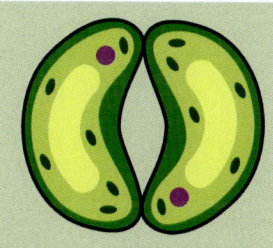

Pathogens and non-specific immunity

Pathogens
All specs except: CCEA

- Pathogens are microorganisms (viruses, bacteria, protists, and fungi) that cause infectious disease.
- There are various ways a disease can be spread in animals and plants:
  - **Direct contact:** spread by physical contact
  - **Transfer of infected fluids:** e.g. blood, saliva, semen
  - **Contaminated water:** travels in unsterilised water
  - **Airborne:** propelled through the air in tiny droplets of water through sneezing and coughing
  - **Food:** pathogens in uncooked or spoiled food
  - **Via another animal:** the animal is called a vector
- The spread of disease can be reduced or **prevented** by:
  - Sterilising water with chemicals or UV light
  - Cooking food thoroughly and preparing it in hygienic conditions
  - Disinfecting surfaces
  - Treating infections, e.g. with antibiotics
  - Vaccination
  - Barrier method of contraception to prevent the spread of sexually transmitted diseases, e.g. condoms
- **Bacteria and viruses** can reproduce rapidly inside the body.
  - Bacteria can produce toxins that damage tissues and cause disease symptoms.
  - Viruses live and reproduce inside cells, causing cell damage.

Non-specific immunity
All specs except: Edexcel, CCEA, Pearson IGCSE

- Humans have non-specific defence systems to prevent pathogens from entering the body:
  - **Skin:** forms a physical barrier to prevent pathogens from entering the body, secretes antimicrobial compounds to kill pathogens, and sheds dead surface skin, which removes pathogens.
  - **Tears and saliva:** contain antibacterial lysozymes, which break down bacterial cell walls.
  - **Nose:** contains hairs acting as a filter, preventing large particles from passing through and producing sticky mucus that traps pathogens and is removed when you blow your nose.
  - **Trachea and bronchi:** lined with ciliated cells and goblet cells to prevent pathogens from entering the lungs. Goblet cells produce mucus to trap pathogens and cilia (tiny hair-like projections) rhythmically beat the mucus up the airway to the back of the throat where it is swallowed.
  - **Stomach:** contains hydrochloric acid, which destroys swallowed pathogens.

Viral diseases
All specs except: Edexcel, Pearson IGCSE

Disease	Symptoms	Transmission	Details
Measles	Fever and red skin rash	**Airborne:** inhalation of droplets from sneezes and coughs	• Complications can be fatal • Most young children are vaccinated against measles
HIV	Initially causes flu-like symptoms	**Transfer of infected fluids:** transfer of bodily fluids (e.g. sex, blood transfusions, drug users sharing needles)	• Unless controlled with antiretroviral drugs, the virus attacks immune cells • Damage to the immune system causes AIDS
Tobacco mosaic virus (TMV)	Distinctive 'mosaic' discolouration on leaves	**Direct contact:** rubbing of leaf against an infected leaf	• Affecting many species of plants including tomatoes • Affects growth of plant due to lack of photosynthesis

Bacterial diseases
All specs except: Edexcel, Pearson IGCSE

Disease	Symptoms	Transmission	Details
Salmonella	Fever, abdominal cramps, vomiting, and diarrhoea	Ingesting spoiled or unhygienic food	• Food poisoning • In the UK, poultry are vaccinated against salmonella to control spread
Gonorrhoea	Thick yellow or green discharge from the vagina or penis and pain when urinating	Sexual contact (STD)	• Was easily treated with penicillin until many resistant strains appeared • Treated with antibiotics and prevented by using barrier method of contraception

Fungal and protist diseases
All specs except: OCR A, Edexcel, WJEC, Pearson IGCSE

Disease	Symptoms	Transmission	Details
Rose black spot (fungal)	Purple/black spots on leaves, which often turn yellow and fall early	Water or wind	• Reduces photosynthesis and thus plant growth • Treated using fungicides and removing infected tissue
Malaria (protist)	Recurrent episodes of fever, which can be fatal	Vector – protist carried by mosquito	• Spread controlled by preventing mosquitos from breeding and using mosquito nets to avoid being bitten

The immune system and drugs

The immune system
- If pathogens make it past the non-specific defence system and enter the body, the immune system will coordinate a response to destroy them.
- White blood cells defend against pathogens by:
  - **Phagocytosis:**

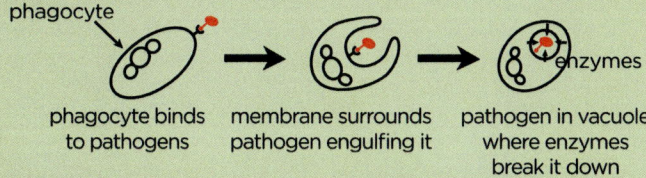

  - **Antibodies:** are specific to each antigen and bind to the antigens of multiple pathogens to clump them together for phagocytosis.
  - **Antibody production:** lymphocytes detect foreign antigens (proteins on surface of cells) on pathogens and respond by producing antibodies.
  - If infected by the same pathogen again, memory lymphocytes recognise the antigens and produce a larger number of specific antibodies faster.
  - **Antitoxin production:** lymphocytes form a special antibody called antitoxins, which bind to and neutralise harmful toxins produced by the pathogen.

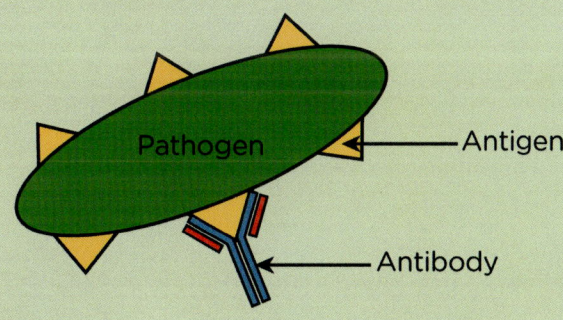

Vaccination
- Vaccination introduces a small amount of dead or inactive forms of a pathogen into the body:
  - This stimulates the production of antibodies.
  - If the pathogen enters the body again, memory lymphocytes will recognise the antigens of the pathogen and produce a larger number of specific antibodies faster.
  - The pathogen is destroyed before the person becomes ill.
- Herd immunity is where the spread of pathogens can be reduced by immunising a large proportion of the population, meaning the disease is unlikely to spread.

Antibiotics
- Antibiotics are medicines used to treat bacterial diseases. For example, penicillin is an antibiotic produced by a fungus, which kills bacteria by weakening their cell walls so they burst.
- Some antibiotics alter bacterial enzymes. Others stop bacteria from reproducing.
- Specific antibiotics are used to kill specific bacteria, and they cannot kill viruses.
- Antibiotics have greatly reduced deaths from bacterial diseases.
- Some strains of bacteria have evolved **resistance to antibiotics.**
- Over-prescription of antibiotics has contributed to the emergence of these resistant strains. Drug companies are constantly researching new antibiotics or alternatives for resistant strains.

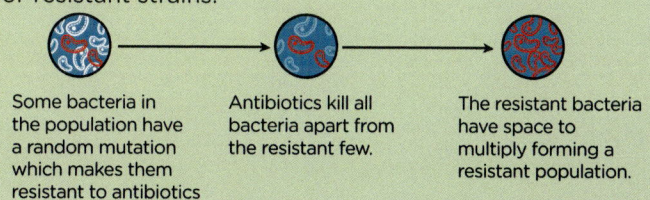

Modern and historical drug development
All specs except: Pearson IGCSE
- Drugs were traditionally extracted from plants and microorganisms. For example, the painkiller aspirin comes from the willow tree, and the heart drug digitalis comes from foxgloves.
- Penicillin was discovered accidentally by Alexander Fleming from the **Penicillium mould**, which contaminated his petri dish of bacteria.
- Most modern drugs are **artificially synthesised** by chemists in the pharmaceutical industry (e.g. paracetamol).
- It is difficult to develop drugs that destroy viruses without also damaging the body's tissues, as viruses are active within human body cells.
- The key stages in modern drug development are:
  - **Identifying a potential drug:** this may be a chemical extracted from another organism like a plant, or a new artificially synthesised chemical combination.
  - **Computer modelling:** investigate the drug's structure and potential interactions with substances in the body.
  - **Preclinical testing:** checks the drugs are safe and effective (e.g. testing for toxicity and efficiency) in a laboratory using live cells, tissues, and animals.
  - **Clinical trials:**
    - First phase uses healthy volunteers to test toxicity.
    - Very low doses of the drug are given at the start of the trial. If the drug is safe, it will be given to a small number of sick patients in phase two to test efficacy.
    - Phase three trials use more patients and finalise safe, optimum doses.
    - In double-blind trials, some patients are given a placebo to test whether the drug is causing the improvement in patients or if it is just the placebo effect.
  - **Manufacturing:** producing the drug on a mass scale to make it publicly available.

Plant disease and monoclonal antibodies

Plant defences

All specs except: WJEC, CIE, Pearson IGCSE

- **Physical defence responses** include:
  - Cellulose cell walls act as a barrier to pathogens.
  - Tough waxy cuticle on leaves to control water loss acts as a barrier to pathogens.
  - Layers of undigestible dead cells around stems (bark on trees) prevent plant being eaten by herbivores, and dead cells falling of sheds pathogens.
- **Chemical plant defence responses** include antibacterial chemicals (e.g. tea tree leaves), or poisons to prevent being eaten by herbivores (e.g. deadly nightshade).
- **Mechanical adaptations** include thorns and spines to prevent being eaten by herbivores, leaves that droop or curl when touched, knocking insects off, and mimicry to trick animals, e.g. some species have spotted leaves that look like butterfly eggs, which prevents butterflies from egg-laying to avoid competition.

Plant diseases

Higher tier
Only: AQA, OCR A, OCR B, Eduqas

- **Symptoms of plant disease** include: stunted growth, spots on leaves, rot (areas of decay), abnormal growths, malformed stem or leaves, discolouration, and pests.
- Plant diseases can be **identified** by researching using a gardening manual or website, taking the infected plant to a laboratory to identify the pathogen, or using monoclonal antibody testing kits.
- Plants can be infected by **insects** or **viral, bacterial, or fungal pathogens.**
  - **Aphids** are insects that tap into the phloem of plant stems with very fine mouthparts (stylet) to ingest the sap. This deprives the plant of its nutrient source. Plant growth rate decreases and the plant wilts. This can be prevented by increasing the number of ladybirds in your garden as they eat aphids, rather than spraying insecticides.
  - **Tobacco mosaic virus:** a viral disease transmitted by infected leaves rubbing against each other, resulting in a mosaic pattern of discoloured leaves. This affects many plant species (e.g. tomatoes) and affects their growth rate by reducing the rate of photosynthesis that can occur.
  - **Black spot:** a fungal disease that is transmitted by water or wind. It results in purple or black spots developing on leaves which are then more likely to turn yellow and fall/die. This affects the growth rate of the plant as photosynthesis is reduced, but can be treated using fungicides and removing/destroying the affected leaves so the disease cannot spread.
- Plants can also be subject to **nutrient deficiencies:**
  - **Mineral ions** are absorbed from the soil by the roots.
  - **Nitrate ions** are needed for protein synthesis and therefore growth. Hence, nitrate deficiency causes stunted growth.
  - **Magnesium ions** are needed to make chlorophyll for photosynthesis. Therefore, magnesium deficiency causes chlorosis (yellow leaves).

Producing monoclonal antibodies

Higher tier
All specs except: CCEA, CIE, Pearson IGCSE

- Monoclonal antibodies are a large population of identical antibodies that are **specific to one protein antigen** and so target a specific chemical or cell in the body. Once the antibody is bound, the target can easily be detected or targeted for treatment.
- Monoclonal antibodies are produced from a **single clone of cells.**
  - An antigen is injected into a mouse. This stimulates the mouse lymphocytes to make an antibody specific to this antigen.
  - The lymphocytes are collected from spleen cells.
  - The lymphocytes are combined with myeloma tumour cells to make **hybridoma cells.**
  - The hybridoma cells are grown in a culture medium indefinitely, where they replicate and produce large amounts of the antibody.
  - The antibody is collected and purified by centrifugation, filtration, and chromatography.

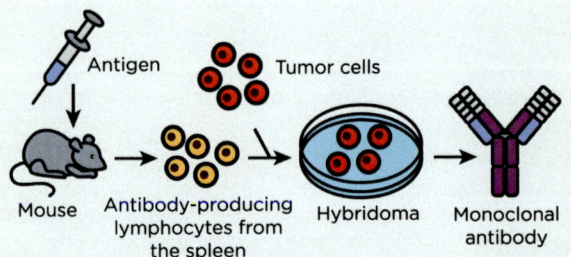

Using monoclonal antibodies

Higher tier
All specs except: CCEA, CIE, Pearson IGCSE

- Monoclonal antibodies have many uses, though they have more side effects than expected, so are not widely used.
- **Pregnancy tests:** HCG is a hormone found in the urine of pregnant people. The person suspecting pregnancy urinates on a small stick of paper containing a strip of monoclonal antibodies specific to HCG. If the person is pregnant, HCG in the urine binds to the antibodies and the test turns colours.
- **Treating disease:** in cancer treatment, the monoclonal antibody is bound to a radioactive substance, toxic drug or chemical, which stops cancerous cells growing and dividing. The antibody binds specifically to the cancer cells, delivering these substances without harming other body cells.
- **Identifying specific molecules:** antibodies can be tagged with a fluorescent dye and are specific to the molecule to be identified/located.
- **Pathogen detection:** monoclonal antibodies can be used to detect pathogens or measure the levels of hormones and chemicals in blood in a laboratory. Antibodies are bound to a fluorescent dye so that when they bind to the antigen and are viewed under UV light, they glow.

Photosynthesis and respiration

Photosynthesis
- Photosynthesis is an endothermic reaction where light energy from the environment is transferred into the chloroplasts.
- Chlorophyll is the green pigment in chloroplasts, which absorb light energy for photosynthesis.
- Photosynthesis is carried out by the plant to produce glucose, which has many uses including plant respiration.
- Word equation: $carbon\ dioxide + water \xrightarrow{light} glucose + oxygen$
- Symbol equation: $CO_2 + H_2O \xrightarrow{light} C_6H_{12}O_6 + 6O_2$

Rate of photosynthesis
- There are various factors that can affect the rate of photosynthesis. These factors interact and the one that limits the reaction rate of photosynthesis is known as the limiting factor, meaning the rate cannot increase without changing that condition.

Factor	Effect on photosynthesis rate
Temperature	• Increases as temperature increases, as molecules have more kinetic energy, so they collide more and react faster. • Decreases at temperatures that are too high as the enzymes involved in photosynthesis denature.
Light intensity	• Increases as light intensity increases, as light energy is needed for the reaction. • If the distance between the plant and light is doubled, the rate is quartered (inverse square law): light intensity ∝ 1/(distance^2)
Carbon dioxide concentration	• Increases as concentration increases, as carbon dioxide is needed for reaction.
Amount of chlorophyll	• Increases as chlorophyll amount increases, as chlorophyll absorbs light energy needed for reaction.

- **Limiting factors** are important in the economics of enhancing the conditions in greenhouses to gain the maximum rate of photosynthesis while still maintaining a profit (e.g. if photosynthesis rate is only limited by the current light intensity, increasing the temperature in the greenhouse will not have a big effect).

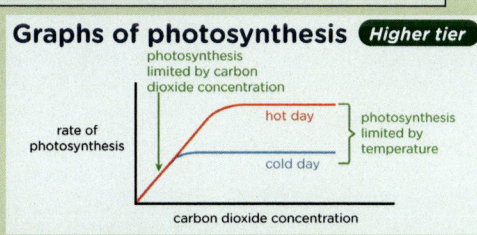

- The **glucose** produced in photosynthesis may be used in:
  ◦ Respiration to provide energy for the plant.
  ◦ Converted into insoluble starch for storage for later use.
  ◦ Producing fat or oil for storage.
  ◦ Producing cellulose, which strengthens the cell wall.
  ◦ Producing amino acids for protein synthesis and growth, which also requires nitrate ions from the soil.

Aerobic respiration
- **Cellular respiration** is an **exothermic** reaction as it releases energy. It continuously occurs in living cells to provide the energy needed for living processes. It is aerobic meaning it **uses oxygen.** Energy is released from glucose by completely oxidising it.
- Word equation: $glucose + oxygen \rightarrow carbon\ dioxide + water$
- Symbol equation: $C_6H_{12}O_6 + 6O_2 \rightarrow 6CO_2 + 6H_2O$

Anaerobic respiration
- Anaerobic respiration takes place **without oxygen.** As it is the incomplete oxidation of glucose, much less energy is released than in aerobic respiration.
- Anaerobic respiration takes place in **muscles in humans.**
  ◦ Word equation: $glucose \rightarrow lactic\ acid$
  ◦ The incomplete oxidation of glucose produces lactic acid.
- Anaerobic respiration takes place in **plant and yeast cells.**
  ◦ Word equation: $glucose \rightarrow ethanol + carbon\ dioxide$
  ◦ Anaerobic respiration in yeast cells is called fermentation and is used in the manufacture of bread and alcoholic drinks.

Metabolism and response to exercise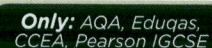
- Metabolism is the sum of all the reactions in a cell or the body. This includes:
  ◦ Respiration and conversion of glucose to starch, glycogen, and cellulose.
  ◦ The formation of lipid molecules from a molecule of glycerol and three molecules of fatty acids.
  ◦ The use of glucose and nitrate ions to form the amino acids for protein synthesis.
  ◦ Digestion (breakdown of carbohydrates, proteins, and lipids)
  ◦ Breakdown of excess proteins to form urea for excretion.
- The energy released by cellular respiration is used by the organism for the continual enzyme-controlled processes of metabolism to synthesise new molecules.
- During exercise, the human body reacts to the increased demand for energy.
- Heart rate, breathing rate and breath volume increase to supply the muscles with more oxygenated blood so they can carry out maximum aerobic respiration to release energy for movement.

Lactic acid accumulation
Higher tier
Only: AQA, Eduqas, Pearson IGCSE
- If insufficient oxygen is supplied, anaerobic respiration takes place in muscles to provide energy, causing a build-up of **lactic acid,** which causes cramps and muscle fatigue, so they stop contracting efficiently.
- Blood flowing through the muscles transports the lactic acid to the liver where it is converted back into glucose. **Oxygen debt** is the amount of extra oxygen required after exercise to react with lactic acid to remove it from cells.

The nervous system and homeostasis

The nervous system
- The nervous system enables humans to react to their surroundings and to coordinate their behaviour.

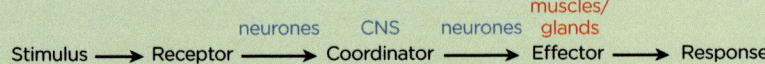

Stimulus → Receptor → Coordinator (neurones, CNS, neurones) → Effector (muscles/glands) → Response

- The stimulus is the change that the body must respond to.
- The receptor is the cell or part of a cell that detects the change and generates an electrical impulse. The information passes along neurone cells as electrical impulses to the central nervous system (CNS) which is made up of the brain and spinal cord and coordinates the response involving effectors.
- The effector response may involve causing muscles to contract or glands to secrete hormones.

Synapses
- Electrical impulses move from one neurone to the next at junctions called synapses.
  - An electrical impulse reaches the end of an axon's branch.
  - The end branches convert the electrical impulse into a chemical signal called neurotransmitters, which diffuse across the synapse.
  - The neurotransmitters bind to the receptors on the dendrites of the neighbouring neurone, triggering the start of an electrical impulse in the neurone.
  - Once bound to receptors, the neurotransmitter is broken down by enzymes to prevent the second neurone from continually sending new electrical impulses.

Reflex arcs
- Reflex actions take place to stop you damaging your body by mistake, in order to prevent or minimise damage, e.g. moving your hand away from a flame when pain and heat receptors sense burning.
- Reflex actions are automatic and rapid as they go through relay neurones in the spinal cord and do not involve the conscious part of the brain, meaning time is not taken sending the information there.
- Reflex responses also occur to coordinate internal processes without conscious thought, e.g. regulate heart rate and controlling pupil size.
- Reaction time is the time it takes to respond to a stimulus.

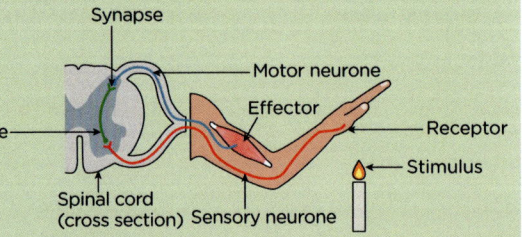

Nerves and neurones
- A bundle of neurones running parallel to each other forms a nerve.
- A fatty layer called the myelin sheath acts as insulation around sensory and motor neurones, speeding up the speed of electrical transmission.

Sensory neurones carry electrical impulses from the receptor to the CNS.	
Relay neurones carry electrical impulses through the CNS.	
Motor neurones carry electrical impulses from the CNS to an effector (muscle or gland).	

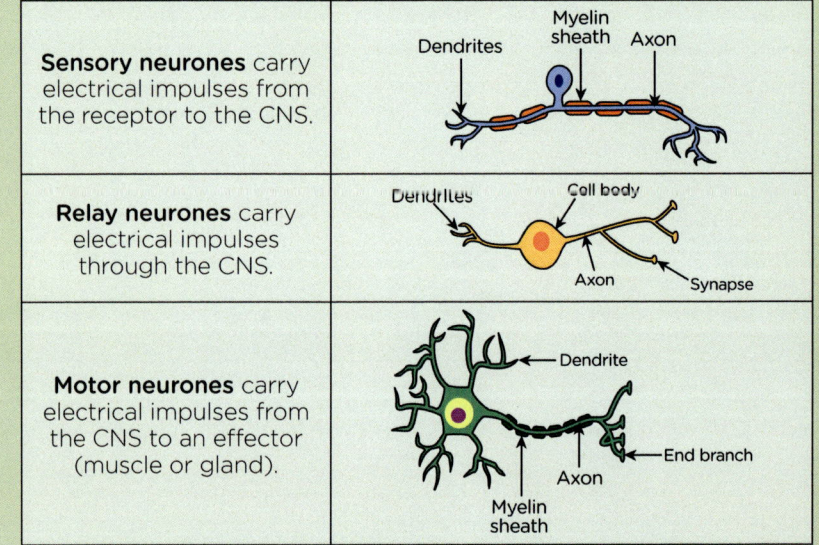

Homeostasis
- Homeostasis is the **regulation of the internal conditions** of a cell or organism to maintain optimum conditions for enzyme activity and all cellular functions in response to internal and external changes.
- In humans, homeostasis includes control of:
  - Blood glucose concentration (too low and you would not release enough energy in respiration, too high and you go into a coma).
  - Body temperature (too low and your enzymes will have a low kinetic energy and reactions would take place too slowly, too high and enzymes would denature and be unable to catalyse reactions).
  - Water levels (too low and your cells will shrink, too high and your cells will burst).
- Automatic control systems, involving nervous or chemical responses, are used to maintain homeostasis. Responses involving the nervous system happen very quickly using electrical impulses, whereas responses involving the hormonal system are slower as the hormones travel in the blood.
- Control systems include **receptor cells,** which detect the stimulus (the change in the environment), **coordination centres,** which receive and process information from receptors (such as the brain, spinal cord, and pancreas), and **effectors,** which bring about responses that restore optimum levels (muscles or glands).

The brain and the eye

The brain
- The brain controls complex behaviour. It is made of billions of interconnected neurones and has different regions that carry out different functions.
- **Cerebral cortex:** divided into left and right hemispheres, responsible for consciousness, memories, intelligence, and the ability to use language.
- **Cerebellum:** controls and coordinates the movements of muscles.
- **Medulla:** controls unconscious/involuntary activities (e.g. heart rate, breathing).

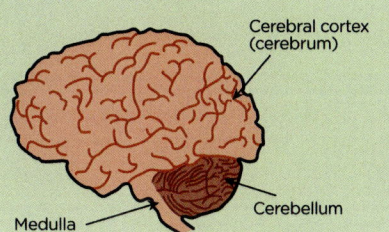

Studying the brain

Higher tier
All specs except: CCEA, WJEC, CIE, Pearson IGCSE

- The complexity and delicacy of the brain make investigating and treating brain disorders difficult. Brain surgery is risky and may cause side effects or further damage, and brain-damaged patients may not be able to consent.
- Neuroscientists have mapped the regions of the brain to particular functions by studying patients with brain damage, using non-invasive techniques, such as electrically stimulating different parts of the brain, and using MRI scanning techniques.

The eye
The eye is a sense organ that contains receptors sensitive to light intensity and colour. Structures in the eye include:
- **Retina:** contains light-sensitive receptor cells: rods and cones that convert light into an electrical impulse. Cones allow you to see in colour when light intensity is high (daytime), while rods work in lower light intensities (night-time) but only enable black and white vision.
- **Optic nerve:** takes electrical impulses from eyes to the brain to generate an 'image'.
- **Sclera:** outer layer that protects the eye (white in humans).
- **Cornea:** transparent layer that refracts light through the pupil.
- **Iris:** muscles surrounding the pupil that control the size of the pupil. Muscles contract and relax to control how much light enters the eye.
- **Lens:** changes shape to focus light on the retina.
- **Ciliary muscles:** contract/relax to change the shape of the lens.
- **Suspensory ligaments:** loosen and tighten to change lens shape.

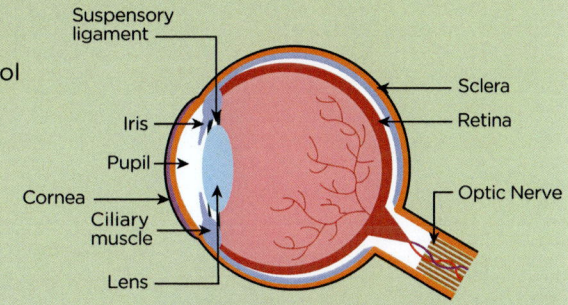

Accommodation and adaptation to dim light

Only: AQA, Edexcel, Pearson IGCSE

- Accommodation is the automatic process of changing the shape of the lens to focus on near or distant objects.
- To focus on a near object:
  - The ciliary muscles contract
  - The suspensory ligaments loosen
  - The lens becomes shorter and thicker, refracting light rays strongly
- To focus on a distant object:
  - The ciliary muscles relax
  - The suspensory ligaments are pulled tight
  - The lens is pulled thinner/longer and only slightly refracts light
- When light intensity is low (e.g. at night) the pupil becomes larger (dilates) in a reflex response to maximise the amount of light entering the eye. The muscles in the iris increase the size of the pupil (dilated pupils), radial muscles contract, and circular muscles relax. The opposite takes place in bright light, to prevent too much light from entering and damaging the eye.

Myopia and hyperopia

All specs except: CCEA, WJEC, CIE, Pearson IGCSE

- Sometimes rays of light do not focus on the retina.
  - **Myopia** is short-sightedness.
  - **Hyperopia** is long-sightedness.
- These defects are treated with spectacle lenses (glasses), which refract the light rays so that they focus on the retina.
- New technologies include hard and soft contact lenses, laser surgery to change the shape of the cornea and a replacement lens in the eye.

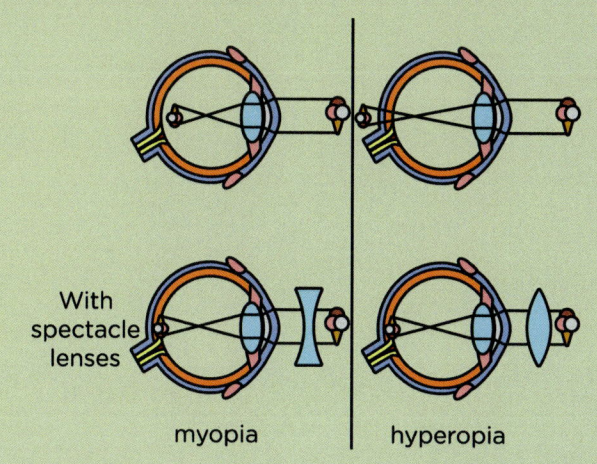

With spectacle lenses

myopia   hyperopia

Hormone regulation and waste excretion

The endocrine system

- The endocrine system is composed of glands, which secrete hormones into the bloodstream.
- The blood carries hormones to target organs where they produce an effect. These effects are slower but longer lasting than in the nervous system.
- The pituitary gland is a 'master gland' found in the brain. It secretes several hormones into the blood in response to body conditions. The hormones it secretes act on other glands to stimulate other hormones to be released.

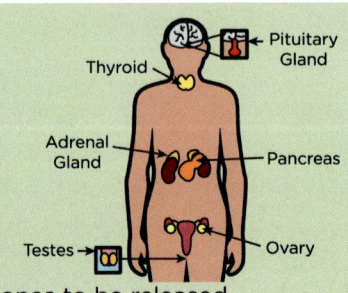

Thermoregulation

- Body temperature is monitored and controlled by the thermoregulatory centre in the brain which contains receptors sensitive to the temperature of the blood.
- The skin contains temperature receptors and sends nervous impulses to the brain.
- If the body temperature is too high arterioles near the skin's surface dilate (vasodilation), increasing blood flow so more heat is lost from the body via convection, conduction, and radiation. Sweat is produced from sweat glands, so energy is taken from the body as it evaporates.
- If the body temperature is too low arterioles near the surface of the skin constrict (vasoconstriction), minimising blood flow and heat loss. Sweating stops, and skeletal muscles involuntarily contract and relax quickly (shiver) to generate heat.

Control of blood glucose and diabetes

- Blood glucose concentration is monitored and controlled by the **pancreas**.
- If the blood glucose concentration is too high, the pancreas produces the hormone **insulin** to return it to normal levels by moving glucose from the blood to the cells. Excess glucose is converted to **glycogen** for storage in liver and muscles.
- If blood glucose is too low, the pancreas produces the hormone **glucagon**, which causes glycogen to be converted into glucose to be released into the blood.
- Control of blood glucose concentration by insulin and glucagon occurs via a **negative feedback cycle** as the body detects a change from the optimum and makes an adjustment to return it back to normal.
- **Type 1 diabetes** is a disorder in which the pancreas fails to produce sufficient insulin. It is characterised by uncontrolled high blood glucose levels and is normally treated with regular insulin injections.
- **In Type 2 diabetes,** the body cells no longer respond to the insulin produced by the pancreas. Obesity is a major risk factor for Type 2 diabetes, and a carbohydrate-controlled diet and an exercise regime are common treatments.

Adrenaline and thyroxine

Higher tier
All specs except: CCEA, WJEC, CIE, Pearson IGCSE

- **Adrenaline** is produced by the **adrenal glands** in times of fear or stress, preparing the body for **'flight or fight,'** increasing heart rate, blood pressure, and blood glucose levels, boosting the delivery of oxygen and glucose to the brain and muscles for respiration. Levels are not controlled by negative feedback.
- **Thyroxine** is produced by the **thyroid gland** and stimulates the **basal metabolic rate.** It plays an important role in growth and development. Levels are controlled by **negative feedback,** maintaining the levels within certain limits.

Water balance and protein removal

- If body cells gain or lose too much water by osmosis, they do not function efficiently. If body fluids become too **dilute,** cells can swell and burst as they take up more water by osmosis. If body fluids are too **concentrated,** cells can shrink as more water leaves by osmosis.
- Uncontrollable water loss can occur via the lungs during exhalation or as water, ions, and urea are lost from the skin in sweat.
- The controlled removal of excess water (to maintain water balance), ions and urea takes place in the kidneys, which produce urine and maintain the water balance.
- The digestion of proteins from the diet results in **excess amino acids.**
- In the liver, excess amino acids are deaminated to form ammonia, which is toxic, so it is converted into urea which travels via plasma to the kidney for excretion.

The kidney

- The kidneys produce urine by filtration of the blood and selective reabsorption of useful substances, such as glucose, water and some ions.
- The water balance in the body is controlled by the hormone **ADH** which increases the permeability of kidney tubules. ADH is released by the pituitary gland when the blood is too concentrated, causing more water to be reabsorbed back into the blood from the kidney tubules (i.e. negative feedback as more ADH is released when the blood is more concentrated).
- Kidney failure happens when a person's kidneys are no longer able to filter their blood effectively and can lead to toxicity. **Kidney dialysis** can be used to treat kidney failure temporarily by the removal of high levels of urea. This involves filtering the blood through a dialysis machine to diffuse urea out of the blood before it is returned to the body.
- An **organ transplant** can be used to treat kidney failure as humans have two kidneys and only require one to survive, so a living person can donate a kidney for transplant.
- The body may treat the kidney as foreign and the body's immune system may attack it. Immunosuppressant drugs are given to the patient to reduce the chances of rejection; however, these weaken their immune system.

Reproductive hormones and plant hormones

Hormones in reproduction and the menstrual cycle

All specs except: WJEC

- During puberty, reproductive hormones cause secondary sex characteristics to develop, e.g. pubic hair.
- **Oestrogen** is the main female reproductive hormone, which is produced in the ovaries. At puberty, eggs begin to mature, and one is released approximately every 28 days (ovulation).
- **Testosterone** is the main male reproductive hormone, produced by testes, stimulating sperm production.
- The menstrual cycle is around 28 days long and requires **oestrogen** and **progesterone** from the ovaries and **follicle-stimulating hormone (FSH)** and **luteinising hormone (LH)** produced by the pituitary gland.
- Several hormones interact in the menstrual cycle to control it:
  - FSH causes maturation of an egg in the ovary and stimulates ovaries to produce oestrogen.
  - Oestrogen thickens the uterus lining in preparation for a fertilised ovum, after menstruation. High oestrogen concentration inhibits the release of FSH and stimulates the release of LH.
  - LH stimulates the release of the egg around day 14.
  - Progesterone maintains the thick uterus lining if a fertilised ovum embeds in it, preventing menstruation. High progesterone concentration inhibits release of FSH and LH.
  - If no fertilised ovum embeds in the uterus lining, less progesterone is produced, and the uterus lining shreds (menstruation). This starts on day 1, lasts approximately 5 days, and marks the start of the cycle.

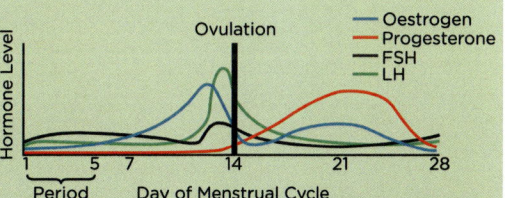

Contraception

All specs except: WJEC

Fertility can be controlled by a variety of hormonal and non-hormonal methods.
- **Hormonal methods:**
  - **Oral contraceptives:** contain oestrogen and progesterone to inhibit FSH production so that no eggs mature. This also thickens mucus in the uterus so it is harder for sperm to travel through, and thins the lining of the uterus so there is less chance of a fertilised ovum embedding.
  - **Injection, implant, or skin patch:** slow-release progesterone to inhibit maturation/release of eggs.
  - **Intrauterine devices:** release progesterone to prevent implantation.
- **Non-hormonal methods:**
  - **Barrier method:** (e.g. condoms, diaphragms) prevent to sperm from reaching an egg.
  - **Spermicidal agents:** often used to coat barrier methods to kill/disable sperm.
  - **Intrauterine devices:** prevent the implantation of an embryo.
  - **Abstaining from intercourse:** no sperm enters the female reproductive system.
  - **Surgical sterilisation:** for males, a vasectomy means sperm ducts are tied or cut; for females, tubal litigation means fallopian tubes are tied or cut.

Infertility

Higher tier
All specs except: WJEC, CIE

- FSH and LH can be artificially provided in fertility drugs to support natural pregnancy through sexual intercourse, such as through **In Vitro Fertilisation (IVF)**
- IVF involves injecting FSH and LH to stimulate the maturation of several eggs. The eggs are collected and fertilised by sperm in vitro (outside the body) in a lab, and the fertilised eggs develop into embryos before being implanted in uterus.
- Fertility treatments allow people to have babies who otherwise might not be able to. However, it is emotionally and physically stressful, can have low success rates, and can lead to multiple births, which are a risk to both the babies and the person giving birth.

Tropisms

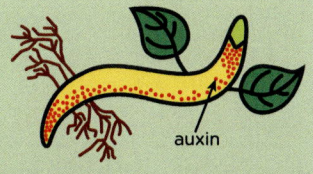

- Plants produce hormones called auxins to coordinate and control growth in response to light (phototropism) and gravity (gravitropism or geotropism).
- Auxins are produced in the tips of shoots and roots.
- Unequal distributions of auxin cause unequal growth rates in plant roots and shoots.
- **Phototropism**:
  - Plant shoots grow towards the light (positive phototropism) to maximise the light absorbed for photosynthesis.
  - In shoots, auxin causes cell elongation.
  - Auxins will concentrate on the shaded side of the shoot, causing unequal growth that makes the shoot bend towards the light.
- **Gravitropism**:
  - Plant roots grow downwards towards water (positive geotropism) in response to gravity, while plant shoots are negatively gravitropic.
  - In roots, auxin slows cell growth on the lower side, causing curvature downwards.

Uses of plant hormones

Higher tier
All specs except: WJEC, CIE, Pearson IGCSE

- Plant growth hormones are used in agriculture and horticulture.
- **Auxins:** used to promote growth in tissue culture.
  - Selective weed killers: broad-leaved weeds, such as dandelions, have a larger surface area to absorb more weed killer, which causes uncontrollable growth of some cells and inhibits growth in others, killing the plant.
  - Rooting powders: plant cuttings are taken, and the cut end of the stem is dipped in rooting powder and placed into the soil where auxin helps the cutting form roots.
- **Ethene** causes the ripening of fruit by controlling cell division. It is involved in the opening of flowers and dropping of leaves.
  - Fruit is often picked before it is ripe to prevent rotting during the long journey to supermarkets, so ethene is sprayed on fruit before arriving so it ripens as it is placed on the shelves.
- **Gibberellins** are involved in plant growth as they initiate seed germination and stem elongation, forming flowers and fruit.
  - This can be used to end seed dormancy to trigger germination, promote flowering, or increase the size of fruit.

Cell division, reproduction, and DNA structure

Mitosis and meiosis
- **Mitosis:** cells divide in a series of stages called the cell cycle.
  - **Stage 1 – Interphase:** cell growth, increase in number of organelles, DNA replicates so there are 2 copies of each chromosome (diploid).
  - **Stage 2 – Mitosis:** one set of chromosomes is pulled to each end of the cell and the nucleus divides.
  - **Stage 3 – Cytokinesis:** cytoplasm and cell membrane divide to form 2 identical daughter cells.
  - Mitosis is important in the growth and development of multicellular organisms. It also replaces old or damaged cells.
- **Meiosis:** cells in reproductive organs divide to form **gametes**, halving the number of chromosomes. Copies of the genetic information are made, and the cell divides twice to form four gametes, each with a single set of chromosomes.
  - All gametes are genetically different from each other. They fuse at fertilisation, forming a zygote and restoring the full number of chromosomes.
  - Meiosis leads to **non-identical cells** being formed.
  - The zygote divides by mitosis, increasing the number of cells to form an embryo, and the cells differentiate as the embryo develops.

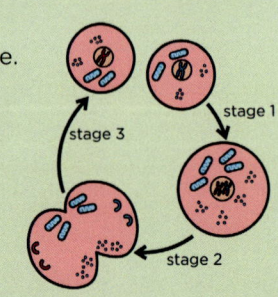

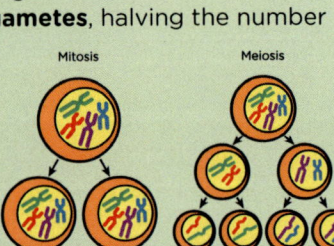

Sexual and asexual reproduction
- **Sexual reproduction** involves the fusion of male and female gametes known as fertilisation (e.g. sperm and egg cells in animals; pollen and egg cells in flowering plants). There is a mixing of genetic information from each parent, which leads to variety in offspring. Advantages of sexual reproduction include:
  - Produces **genetic variation** in offspring. If the environment changes, variation gives a survival advantage by natural selection due to adaptations.
  - Natural selection can be sped up by humans through **selective breeding** (e.g. breeding the best plants to increase food production).
- **Asexual reproduction** involves only one parent and no fusion of gametes, so there is no mixing of genetic information (e.g. prokaryotic bacteria reproduce asexually). Mitosis occurs, which produces cells that are genetically identical (clones) to the parent cell. Advantages of asexual reproduction include:
  - Only one parent needed, so the process is more **time and energy-efficient** than sexual reproduction as individuals do not need to find a mate.
  - Many identical offspring can be produced in favourable conditions.
- Some organisms can reproduce by both sexual and asexual reproduction (e.g. runners in strawberry plants, bulb division in daffodils, malarial parasites reproducing asexually in the human host and sexually in the mosquito, and fungi reproducing asexually by spores and sexually to give variation).

DNA
- The genetic material in the nucleus of a cell is made up of a chemical called **DNA** which is made up of two strands forming a **double helix**.
- The DNA is contained in structures called **chromosomes**, and a **gene** is a small section of DNA on a chromosome.
- Each gene codes for a sequence of **amino acids** that makes a specific **protein**.
- The **genome** is the entire genetic material of an organism.

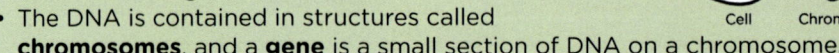

DNA structure
- DNA is made from repeating nucleotide units consisting of alternating sugar and phosphate groups with the sugar attached to one of four bases.
- DNA contains four different bases: A, C, G, and T.
- A sequence of three bases is the code for a particular amino acid, so the order determines the assembly of proteins.
- Two DNA strands form a double helix; the strands are complementary and bind to a specific base on the opposite strand via hydrogen bonds:
  - C always binds to a G.
  - T always binds to an A.

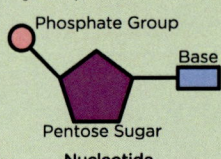

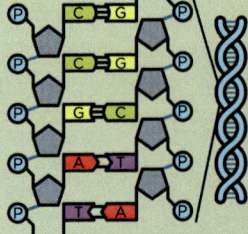

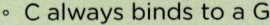

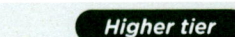

Gene expression and mutations *Higher tier*
- Not all parts of DNA code for proteins. **Non-coding** parts of DNA play a role in gene expression and can switch genes on and off. **Variations** in non-coding regions may affect how genes are expressed.
- A **mutation** is a change in the DNA sequence; for example, an insertion of a nucleotide or a deletion of one.
- Mutations occur continuously, but most mutations do not alter the protein or only alter it slightly so that its shape and therefore function is not changed.
- A few mutations code for an altered protein with a different shape, altering the activity of a protein, e.g. an enzyme may no longer fit the substrate-binding site or a structural protein may lose its strength.
- Some mutations are advantageous and allow genetic variation.

The Human Genome Project *Only: AQA, Edexcel, WJEC, Eduqas*
- In the Human Genome Project, the sequence of all the bases in the entire human genome was identified using the DNA of male and female volunteers.
- This has advantages in linking genes to different types of diseases, improving our understanding and treatment of inherited disorders, and tracing historical human migration patterns.

DNA synthesis and inheritance

Transcription

Higher tier

- Transcription is the first stage of protein synthesis and takes place in the nucleus.
- An mRNA template is formed from a section of one of the nucleotide strands making up DNA.
- The template formed covers a section of DNA that codes for a particular protein (a gene).

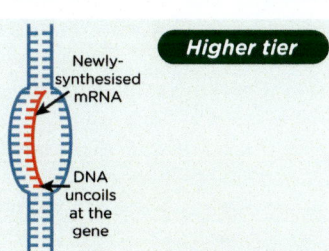

Translation

Higher tier

- Translation is the second stage of protein synthesis and takes place on ribosomes.
- tRNA carrier molecules bring amino acids that are specific to the template.
- A sequence of three bases on the template is the code for an amino acid. Therefore, the order of bases controls the order in which the amino acids are assembled and determines the protein that is made.
- The amino acids brought to the template bind to each other, forming a growing protein chain in the correct order.
- When the protein chain is complete, it folds up to form a unique shape.
- The shape of a protein enables it to do its job as an enzyme or hormone or allows it to form a structure in the body (e.g. collagen).

Inheritance terminology

- **Gene:** a section of DNA that codes for a particular protein.
- **Allele:** two versions of the same gene located at the same place on a chromosome.
- **Gamete:** sex cells that contain half the number of chromosomes of all other cells with male and female gametes combining in fertilisation.
- **Chromosome:** structures of DNA found in the nucleus of eukaryotic cells.
- **Dominant:** an allele that is always expressed, so a characteristic will show if inherited from either parents. Dominant alleles are written as capitals (e.g. 'B' for brown eyes).
- **Recessive:** an allele that will only be expressed and show a characteristic if two copies are present, one from each parent. Recessive alleles are written as lower case letters (e.g. 'b' for blue eyes).
- **Homozygous:** a genotype with two of the same alleles (e.g. 'BB' or 'bb').
- **Heterozygous:** a genotype with two different alleles (e.g. 'Bb').
- **Genotype:** the collection of genes/alleles present in an organism.
- **Phenotype:** the physical characteristics of an organism, determined by the genotype and environment (e.g. if the genotype is Bb, the phenotype is brown eyes).
- **Polygenetic inheritance:** some characteristics are controlled by a single gene (e.g. fur colour in mice, red-green colour blindness in humans) but most characteristics are a result of the interaction of multiple genes, rather than a single gene.

Punnett squares and family trees

- A Punnett square is a grid used to determine the probability of an offspring's genotype based on the genotype of the parents, showing the potential allele combinations offspring can inherit.
- For example, when determining the inheritance of eye colour if both parents have the brown eye phenotype and the genotype Bb:

		Parent 1	
		B	b
Parent 2	B	BB	Bb
	b	Bb	bb

- Genotype ratio BB:Bb:bb = 1:2:1
- Probability of offspring: BB = 25%, Bb = 50%, bb = 25%
- Probability of offspring: Brown eyes = 75%, blue eyes 25%
- Family trees show the inheritance of characteristics over several generations. The oldest members of a family are at the top of a tree, and each new tier represents a new generation. People with XY chromosomes are represented by squares and people with XX chromosomes are represented by circles. Individuals with a specific characteristic will have their shape coloured in, unless shown otherwise with a key.

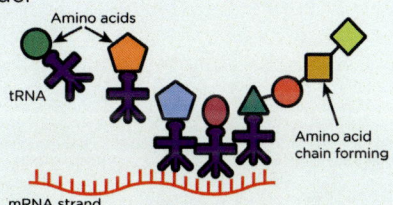

Determining sex

- Ordinary human body cells contain 23 pairs of chromosomes. 22 of these pairs are **somatic cells** that control characteristics. The other 1 pair are **germ-line cells** that carry the genes that determine sex. In females, the sex chromosomes are the same (XX), whereas in males, the sex chromosomes are different (XY).
- Genotype ratio XX:XY = 1:1
- Probability of offspring: XX = 50%, XY = 50%

		Mother	
		X	X
Father	X	XX	XX
	Y	XY	XY

Inherited disorders

Only: AQA, Edexcel, WJEC, CCEA

- Some disorders are caused by the inheritance of certain alleles (e.g. **polydactyly** (having extra fingers or toes) is caused by a dominant allele; **cystic fibrosis** (a disorder of cell membranes) is caused by a recessive allele).
- Embryo screening involves looking for genetic disorders in embryos before they develop, allowing the parents to make an informed decision about continuing or terminating the pregnancy, which may alleviate suffering. However, there is a possible risk to the embryo, and the person carrying the embryo. It is also often expensive, and can be seen as unethical or against some religions.

Genetic engineering and modification

Selective breeding
All specs except: WJEC

- Selective breeding (artificial selection) is the process by which humans breed plants and animals for particular genetic characteristics.
- Humans have been doing this for thousands of years, e.g. the breeding of food crops from wild plants and the domestication of animals.
- Selective breeding involves:
  - Choosing parents with a desired characteristic from a mixed population and breeding them together.
  - Choosing the offspring with the desired characteristic and breeding them together.
  - Repeating the cycle over many generations until all offspring show the desired characteristic.
- The characteristic can be chosen for its usefulness or appearance:
  - Animals that produce more meat or milk.
  - Disease resistance or increased size in food crops.
  - Domestic dogs with a gentle nature.
  - Large or unusual flowers.
- Disadvantages of selective breeding:
  - Can lead to 'inbreeding' when the parents are genetically very similar, where some breeds are especially prone to inherited defects or disease.
  - Reduced genetic variation means that a change in the environment or a disease is more likely to kill an entire population.
  - Physical problems in organisms, e.g. cows weighed down by large udders.
  - The breeding method (e.g. artificial insemination) can be seen as unethical.

Genetic engineering
All specs except: WJEC

- Genetic engineering is the process of modifying the genome of an organism by introducing a gene from another organism to give a desired characteristic.
  - Enzymes are used to isolate the required gene by cutting it from the DNA.
  - The gene is inserted into a vector (a bacterial plasmid or virus). If the vector is a bacterial plasmid, the same enzyme is used to cut open the plasmid and a second is used to seal it.
  - The vector is used to insert the gene into the required cells.
- Genes are transferred to the cells of animals, plants or bacteria at an early stage in their development (e.g. embryo in animals) so they develop with the desired characteristics; all cells produced via mitosis will then contain the same gene.
- Some people disagree with genetic engineering for religious or moral reasons.

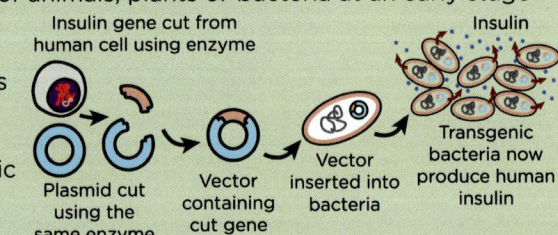

Genetically modified (GM) organisms
All specs except: WJEC

- GM crops can be genetically engineered to improve resistance to diseases and insect attacks, improve resistance to environmental conditions (e.g. drought), produce bigger and better fruit and vegetables, or make crops resistant to the herbicides used on weeds.
- Concerns of GM crops include fears that the genes might spread into the wild gene pool (e.g. herbicide-resistant weeds) and caution about the effects of eating GM crops on human health.

Genetically modified animals and bacteria
Higher tier
Only: AQA, Eduqas, CCEA

- Animals can be genetically engineered to produce necessary molecules (e.g. sheep engineered to produce proteins used in medicine).
- Modern medical research in animals is exploring the possibility of genetic modification to overcome some inherited disorders.
- Bacterial cells have been genetically engineered to produce useful substances, such as human insulin to treat diabetes.
- This enables bacteria to produce insulin at a high yield and produces human insulin, which is safer to use than pig or cattle insulin. However, some people are cautious of the effects of using GM medicines on human health.

Cloning
Only: AQA, Edexcel, CIE

- Cloning is the asexual reproduction or artificial reproduction of an organism to produce genetically identical offspring or organism. For example, plant cloning can be used to grow identical new plants.
- **Methods of plant cloning:**
  - **Tissue culture:** taking small groups of cells from part of a plant and placing them in a growth medium to grow identical new plants. This is used commercially in nurseries or to preserve rare plant species.
  - **Cuttings:** this is an older and simpler method used by gardners whereby offcuts of a plant are treated with plant hormones and placed in soil to develop roots.
- **Animal cloning via embryo transplants:**
  - Cells from a developing embryo are taken before they become specialised.
  - The cells are split from each other and transplanted into the wombs of multiple host animals, and the separated cells develop into identical embryos, forming multiple identical offspring.
  - This is illegal in humans.
- **Adult cell cloning:** when the embryo is a ball of cells, it is inserted into the womb of an adult animal to continue its development. The embryo contains the same genetic information as the adult body cell whose nucleus was inserted into the ovum.

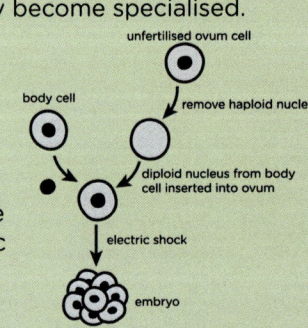

Evolution and natural selection

Variation

- Differences in the characteristics of individuals in a population are called variation.
- The phenotype of an organism is determined by the genome and the genome's interaction with the environment.
  - Some characteristics are determined purely from inherited genes (e.g. biological sex and blood group) and some purely by the environment (e.g. tattoos, scars).
  - Some characteristics are determined by genetics and the environment, where genetics predetermines the potential for a characteristic and the environment determines how much of this potential is reached (e.g. intelligence).
- There is usually extensive genetic variation within a population of a species.
- All genetic variation arises from mutations. Most mutations have no effect on the phenotype, and very few mutations determine phenotype. If the new phenotype is better suited to an environmental change, it can lead to a rapid change in the species.

Evolution

- The theory of evolution states that all species of living things have evolved from simple life forms that first developed over 3 billion years ago.
- Evolution is a change in the inherited characteristics of a population over time through a process called natural selection.
- Natural selection of variants in a population gives rise to phenotypes best suited to their environment and may result in the formation of new species.
- If two populations of a species become so different from each other in phenotype that they can no longer interbreed to produce fertile offspring, they have formed two new species.

Theory of evolution by natural selection

- Charles Darwin proposed his theory of evolution by natural selection based on observations he made on a round-the-world expedition, and developing knowledge of geology and fossils.
- Darwin published his theory in On the Origin of Species (1859). This was controversial at the time for challenging the idea that God made all animals and plants that live on Earth. There was insufficient evidence at the time the theory was published as the mechanisms of inheritance and variation were not known until 50 years after the theory was published.
- Jean-Baptiste Lamarck proposed an earlier theory of evolution that changes that occur in an organism during its lifetime can be inherited. We now know that in the vast majority of cases this type of inheritance cannot occur.
- The theory of evolution by natural selection states that individuals with characteristics most suited to their environment are more likely to survive long enough to breed successfully. The characteristics that have enabled these individuals to survive are passed onto their offspring, and the cycle continues from one generation to the next.

Evidence for evolution

Only: AQA, OCR A, Eduqas

- Evidence for Darwin's theory of evolution by natural selection includes fossil records, inheritable characteristics in humans, and antibiotic resistance in bacteria.
- Fossils are the 'remains' of organisms from millions of years ago, which are found in rocks and show us how much or how little different organisms have changed as life developed on Earth, providing evidence for Darwin's theory of evolution by natural selection. Fossils may be formed from parts of organisms that have not decayed because one or more of the conditions needed for decay are absent (e.g. warmth, air, and moisture), or when parts of the organism are replaced by minerals as they decay. They can also be preserved traces of organisms (e.g. footprints, burrows).
- Scientists cannot be certain about how life began on Earth as many early forms of life were soft-bodied, meaning that they have left few traces behind. Other traces that have been left behind have mainly been destroyed by geological activity.

Mendelian genetics

All specs except: WJEC, CIE, Pearson IGCSE

- In the mid-19th century, Gregor Mendel carried out breeding experiments on plants. He observed that the inheritance of each characteristic was determined by 'units' that were passed on to the descendants unchanged.
  - Mendel studied the inheritance of traits in pea plants to form the laws of Mendelian inheritance. For example, crossing a yellow pea plant with a green pea plant always produced a yellow pea plant, so yellow was found to be dominant and green is recessive. These laws are followed when we carry out Punnett squares to determine the potential genotypes of offspring.
- The importance of Mendel's work was not recognised until after his death as little was known about genetic information at the time; most scientists still believed in blended inheritance where all characteristics are passed on.
  - **Late 19th century:** chromosome behaviour during cell division was first observed.
  - **Early 20th century:** chromosomes and Mendel's 'units' observed to behave in similar ways, leading to the idea that the 'units', later known as genes, were located on chromosomes.
  - **Mid-20th century:** DNA structure and the mechanism of gene function were determined, leading to the development of gene theory.

Solving antibiotic resistance

- Bacteria reproduce at a fast rate so can evolve rapidly, and mutations of bacterial pathogens produce new strains. Some strains might be resistant to antibiotics, so they survive and reproduce, increasing the population of resistant strains (e.g. MRSA).
- To reduce the rate of development of antibiotic-resistant strains, doctors should not prescribe antibiotics inappropriately, such as treating non-serious or viral infections. Patients should always complete their course of antibiotics so that all bacteria are killed and none survive to mutate and form resistant strains, and the agricultural use of antibiotics should be restricted.

Species and classification

Speciation

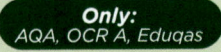
Only: AQA, OCR A, Eduqas

- Though Darwin is more widely appreciated, Alfred Russel Wallace independently proposed a theory of evolution by natural selection as well.
  - He published joint writings with Darwin in 1858.
  - This prompted Darwin to publish On the Origins of Species in 1859.
  - Wallace worked worldwide gathering evidence for evolutionary theory.
- He is best known for his pioneering theory of speciation and his work on warning colouration in animals.
- More evidence over time has led to our current understanding of the theory of speciation, the gradual formation of a new species as a result of evolution.
  - A population of a species is isolated in a different environment to the rest of the species.
  - Different characteristics will be favourable for the survival of individuals in the isolated population as they are in a different environment to the rest of the species.
  - The isolated population will evolve different characteristics to the rest of the species thanks to natural selection.
  - Over time, the isolated population becomes so different from the rest of the species that they can no longer interbreed to form fertile offspring, so the isolated population has formed its own species.
- **Evolutionary trees** are a method used by scientists to show how they believe organisms are related. These trees use current classification data for living organisms and fossil data for extinct organisms.

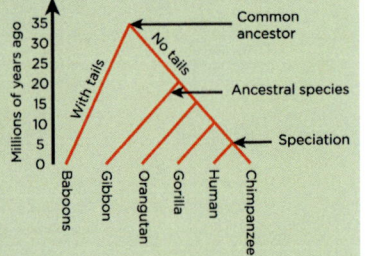

Adaptations

- Organisms have features called adaptations that enable them to survive in the conditions in which they normally live.
  - **Structural adaptations** are physical features (e.g. tigers have sharp teeth to allow them to kill their prey).
  - **Behavioural adaptations** are behaviours that benefit an organism (a courtship display to attract a mate).
  - **Functional adaptations** are physiological processes organisms complete to aid survival (e.g. producing venom to deter predators from killing them).
- Adaptations allow organisms to outcompete others and provide them with an evolutionary advantage.
- Organisms called **extremophiles** live in environments that are very extreme.
  - Extreme conditions include extremely hot or cold temperatures, high pressure or salt concentration, and highly acidic or alkaline environments.
  - For example, bacteria living in deep-sea hydrothermal vents are extremophiles evolved to feed on the sulfur compounds released by the vents, toxic to almost all other life.

Classification and Linnaeus

All specs except: CCEA

- Traditionally, living things have been classified into groups depending on their structure and characteristics.
- This system was developed by Carl Linnaeus.
  - Linnaeus classified living things into kingdom, phylum, class, order, family, genus, and species.
  - Organisms are named by the two-part binomial system of genus plus species.
  - Scientists write binomial names in italics with a capital letter for the genus, e.g. for the organism *Homo sapiens*, *Homo* is the genus and *sapiens* is the species.

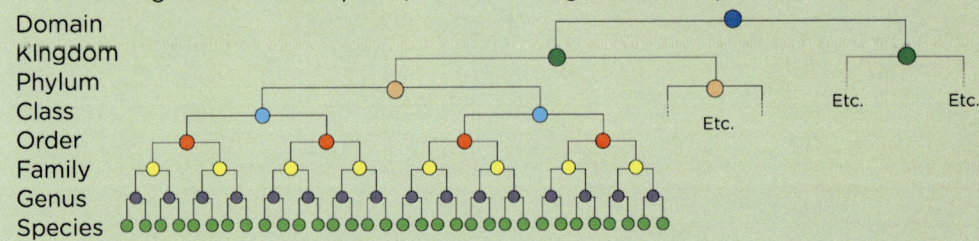

Updates to classification

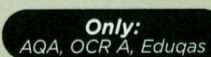
Only: AQA, OCR A, Eduqas

- New models of classification have been proposed due to:
  - Developing evidence of internal structures due to improvements in microscopes.
  - Increased understanding of biochemical processes.
  - Development of techniques such as genome mapping.
- Due to evidence available from chemical analysis, there is now a 'three-domain system' developed by Carl Woese. In this system, organisms are divided into:
  - Archaea (primitive bacteria usually living in extreme environments).
  - Bacteria (true bacteria).
  - Eukaryota (including animals, plants, protists, and fungi).

Extinction

Only: AQA, Eduqas, CCEA

- Extinctions occur when there are no remaining individuals of a species still alive.
- Species that do not successfully adapt to environmental conditions or lack the genetic variation to survive changes in the environment are more likely to go extinct.
- Factors that may contribute to the extinction of a species:
  - Increasing population of humans increases human impact on the environment (e.g. cutting down rainforests, building bigger cities and urban areas, or drilling for oil and minerals).
  - Natural changes over time, e.g. end of the ice age.
  - Introduction of new predators.

Ecosystems

Competition

- An ecosystem is the interaction of a community of **living organisms (biotic)** with the **non-living (abiotic)** parts of their environment.
- To survive and reproduce:
  - Organisms require a supply of materials from their surroundings and from the other living organisms there.
  - Organisms are adapted to the conditions in which they live.
- Organisms compete with each other for multiple factors:
  - Plants often compete for light, space, and for water and mineral ions from soil.
  - Animals often compete for food, mates, and territory.
- Competition between organisms provides a struggle for existence, which drives evolution. Only the organisms best adapted to their environment will survive and reproduce, forming offspring also adapted to their environment. This is known as survival of the fittest.
  - **Interspecific competition** is between different species in a community.
  - **Intraspecific competition** is between organisms of the same species.

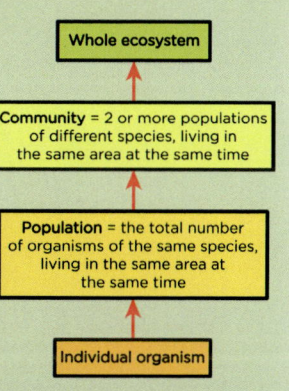

Interdependence

- Within a community, each species depends on other species for food, shelter, pollination, seed dispersal, etc.
- A stable community is one where all the species and environmental factors are in balance with each other so that population sizes remain relatively constant.
- If one species is removed or added it can affect the whole community due to interdependence.

Sampling

- Sampling is the process scientists use to look at a section of a habitat and draw conclusions about the whole of it studied.
- The section of the habitat studied must be large enough to be representative of the whole of it for accurate predictions to be made.
- A range of experimental methods using **transects** (a straight line through the habitat) and **quadrats** (a frame of square grids) are used by ecologists to assess the distribution and abundance of species in an ecosystem.
- Methods of measuring the abundance of organisms:
  - **Mode:** the value that appears most frequently in a data set.
  - **Median:** the middle number in a data set when displayed in ascending order.
  - **Mean (average):** the sum of terms divided by the number of terms.

Biotic and abiotic factors

- **Biotic (living) factors** that can affect a community include availability of food, new predators arriving, new pathogens, or one species outcompeting another so the numbers are no longer sufficient to breed.
  - A change in a biotic factor would affect a community, e.g. if a new pathogen appeared and killed an entire species, the organisms depending on this species for food or a habitat would also die.
- Abiotic (non-living) factors that can affect a community include: **light intensity** (e.g. plants adapted to the shade may quickly wilt and die if they are moved into direct sunlight), **temperature** (e.g. some organisms like reptiles cannot regulate their own body temperature), CO_2 **levels in plants** (a major limiting factor in photosynthesis) and O_2 **levels for aquatic animals** (required for respiration), moisture levels, soil pH and mineral content, and wind intensity/direction.
  - A change in an abiotic factor would affect a community (e.g. cacti are adapted to survive with little water and will die if overwatered, so species that depend on cacti for a habitat or a food resource would then also die).

Predation

- **Predation** is a biological interaction where one organism (the predator) hunts, kills, and eats another organism (the prey). This is a key factor in controlling population sizes in ecosystems.
- Predators often have adaptations such as sharp teeth, claws, camouflage, speed, and keen senses (e.g. sight, smell) to catch prey effectively, whereas prey will have adaptations to avoid detection or capture such as warning colouration, defensive behaviour, camouflage, or speed.
- Predation helps maintain population balance and biodiversity in ecosystems by preventing any one species from becoming too dominant.
- **Predator-prey cycling:**
  - In a stable community, the numbers of predators and prey rise and fall in interdependent cycles.
  - If the number of predators increases, the number of prey decrease after a short lag phase, as more are eaten.
  - As the number of prey decrease, the number of predators will decrease as there is less food.
  - This then causes the number of prey to increase, resulting in an increase in predators.

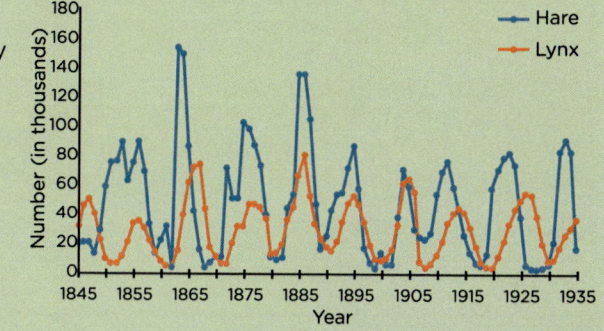

Resource cycles and environmental change

The carbon cycle
- Many different materials cycle through the abiotic and biotic components of an ecosystem.
- All materials in the living world are recycled to provide the building blocks for future organisms
- The carbon cycle is important so that living organisms can continually be supplied with carbon in forms suitable for use in making the molecules necessary for life (e.g. proteins, carbohydrates, lipids, nucleic acids).
- The carbon cycle returns carbon from organisms to the atmosphere as carbon dioxide to be used by plants in photosynthesis.
- Microorganisms are important decomposers that cycle materials through an ecosystem by returning carbon to the atmosphere as carbon dioxide and mineral ions to the soil.

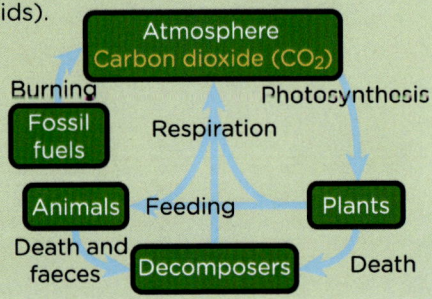

The water cycle
- The water cycle is important so that living organisms can continually be supplied with water, which is the major component of all cells and is thus necessary for life.
- The water cycle provides fresh water for plants and animals on land before draining into the seas.
- Water is continuously evaporated and precipitated (as rain, snow, hail or sleet).
- **Runoff** is the movement of water across the surface.
- **Infiltration** is the movement of water into the ground to become groundwater.
- **Subsurface flow** is the movement of groundwater to the ocean.

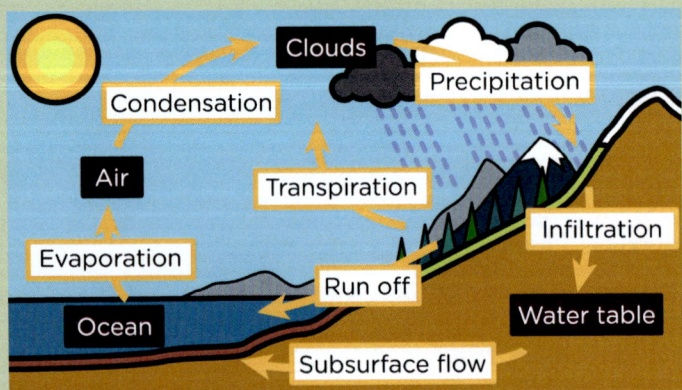

Effects of environmental change
Higher tier
Only: AQA, OCR A, Eduqas, CCEA

Environmental changes affect the distribution of species in an ecosystem and may be seasonal, geographic, or caused by human interaction.

Change	Explanation	Example
Temperature	Enzymes have an optimum temperature at which they function.	**Seasonal:** seasonal decreases in temperature can cause migrations, e.g. towards winter, birds, such as swallows, migrate south from Northern Europe toward hotter temperatures.
Availability of water	No life can exist without water.	**Geographic:** in deserts, cacti and camels have adapted to survive with minimal water, and most life and green plants are found surrounding oases (where water rises from underground sources). The distribution of algal species also varies depending on the tide.
Composition of atmospheric gases	Combustion of fossil fuels release gases that can be toxic to organisms (e.g. oxides of carbon, sulfur and nitrogen).	**Human interaction:** most lichens will only grow in high numbers in clear air as they are sensitive to air pollution. The distribution of species can be a useful bioindicator of air pollution.

Global warming
All specs except: Edexcel, WJEC, Eduqas

- Global warming is the increase in the average temperature of the Earth.
- Levels of carbon dioxide and methane (greenhouse gases) in the atmosphere are increasing and contribute to global warming by trapping more heat.
- The increased emission of greenhouse gases in recent years is due to human activity (e.g. fossil fuel combustion).
- Biological consequences of global warming:
  - Glaciers are melting in the arctic, causing sea levels to rise and a loss of coastal regions and some islands.
  - Loss of suitable habitats for species, causing decreased biodiversity and decreased food security for humans.
  - Extreme weather conditions (e.g. flash floods and droughts).
  - Species are migrating as current conditions are no longer suitable for them.

Biodiversity and environmental management

Biodiversity

- Biodiversity is the variety of all the different species of organisms on earth, or within an ecosystem.
- A great biodiversity ensures the stability of ecosystems by reducing the dependence of one species on another for food, shelter, and the maintenance of the physical environment
- The future of the human species on Earth relies on us maintaining a good level of biodiversity.
- Many human activities are reducing biodiversity (e.g. deforestation) and only recently have measures been taken to try to stop this reduction.

Maintaining biodiversity

Negative effects of humans on ecosystems and biodiversity	Strategies to reduce negative impacts of humans on ecosystems and biodiversity
Deforestation increases global warming and destroys species' habitats	Protection and regeneration of rare habitats, such as rainforests
Burning fossil fuels increases global warming and industrial processes pollute air and habitats with waste chemicals	Reduction of deforestation and carbon dioxide emissions by some governments
Build-up of plastic rubbish in the oceans	Recycling resources rather than dumping waste in landfills
Overfishing damages wild food chains	Quotas on fishing
Oil spills can kill aquatic organisms and species (e.g. sea birds, sea otters, seals)	Breeding programmes for endangered species to promote reproduction varied gene pool

Land use

Only: AQA

- Humans reduce the amount of land available for other animals and plants by building, quarrying, farming, and dumping waste.
- The destruction of peat bogs and other areas of peat may occur to produce garden compost:
  - Peat is made up of partially decayed vegetation.
  - Destruction reduces the area of this habitat and the variety of different species living there (biodiversity).
  - The decay or burning of the peat releases carbon dioxide into the atmosphere.

Deforestation

Only: AQA, Edexcel, CIE

- Large-scale deforestation in tropical areas has occurred to:
  - Provide land for cattle and rice fields.
  - Grow crops for biofuels.
- Environmental implications of deforestation:
  - Increase in carbon dioxide in the atmosphere as there are fewer trees to take in carbon dioxide for photosynthesis.
  - Burning of trees increases atmospheric carbon dioxide.
  - Reduces biodiversity as it destroys species of tree and removes habitat for several species of animals.
  - Causes drier climates as there is less transpiration by trees, resulting in drier soils, fewer roots, and greater risk of erosion and landslides.

Waste management

Only: AQA, Edexcel, CIE

- Increasingly more resources are being used and more waste is being produced due to:
  - Rapid growth in the human population.
  - An increase in the standard of living.
- Unless waste and chemical materials are properly handled, more pollution will be caused.
- Pollution kills plants and animals, which can reduce biodiversity.
- Pollution can occur:
  - In water: from sewage, fertiliser, or toxic chemicals.
  - In air: from smoke and acidic gases.
  - On land: from landfill and toxic chemicals.

Decomposition

- Decomposition is the breakdown of substances into smaller substances, carried out by bacteria and fungi.
- Increasing temperature, oxygen and water availability increases the rate of decay of biological material as bacteria and fungi grow faster.
- The rate change in the decay of biological material is equal to the change in value divided by time.
- Gardeners and farmers try to provide optimum conditions (e.g. neutral pH) for rapid decay of waste biological material to produce compost.
- Compost is used as a natural fertiliser.
- Anaerobic decay produces methane gas, which can be carried out in a biogas generator to produce fuel.

Biomass and trophic levels

Pyramids of biomass

- Biomass is the mass of any living or recently dead organism in grams or kilograms.
- Organisms can gain energy from consuming biomass and turn this energy into their body tissue (their own biomass).
- Dead organisms are first dried in an oven before biomass is recorded as different organisms contain different amounts of water.
- Pyramids of biomass can be constructed to represent the relative amount of biomass in each level of a food chain.
- Trophic level 1 is at the bottom of the pyramid.

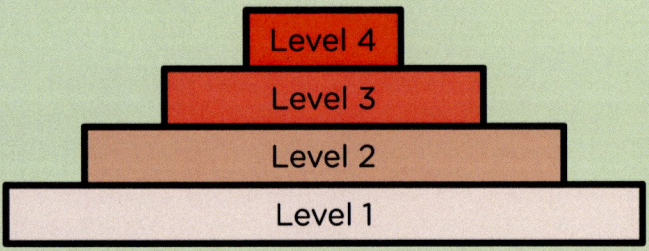

Transfer of biomass

- A pyramid of biomass is largest at the bottom and decreases as we go up the levels as biomass is lost between the different trophic levels.
  ◦ Not all ingested material is absorbed, some is egested as faeces.
  ◦ A lot of absorbed material is lost as waste, such as carbon dioxide and water in respiration and water and urea in urine.
  ◦ Large amounts of glucose are used in respiration.
- Efficiency of biomass transfers is equal to the biomass in the higher trophic level divided by the biomass of the lower trophic level.
- Producers transfer about 1% of the incident energy from light (from the sun) for photosynthesis.
- Only approximately 10% of the biomass from each trophic level is transferred to the level above it.
- As biomass and energy are lost at each level up the food chain, often the number of organisms decreases from one trophic level to the next.
- However, if level 2 was larger than level 1, then the herbivores may eat all of the plants, affecting the food chain.

Food chains and trophic levels

- Feeding relationships within a community can be represented by food chains.
- All food chains begin with a producer, which synthesises molecules (usually a green plant or algae) that makes glucose via photosynthesis. Producers are eaten by **primary consumers**, which may be eaten by **secondary consumers** and then **tertiary consumers.**
- Trophic levels refer to the position an organism occupies in a food chain. Trophic levels can be represented by numbers according to how far an organism is along the food chain.
  ◦ **Level 1: producers** like plants and algae make their own food via photosynthesis.
  ◦ **Level 2: primary consumers** are herbivores that eat producers.
  ◦ **Level 3: secondary consumers** are carnivores or herbivores that eat primary consumers.
  ◦ **Level 4: tertiary consumers** are carnivores that eat secondary consumers.
  ◦ **Apex predators:** are at the top of the food chain and have no predators.
- **Decomposers:** break down dead plant and animal matter by secreting enzymes into the environment. Small soluble food molecules then diffuse into the microorganism. This also releases mineral ions and nutrients that plants can absorb from the soil. Examples include bacteria, fungi, and worms.

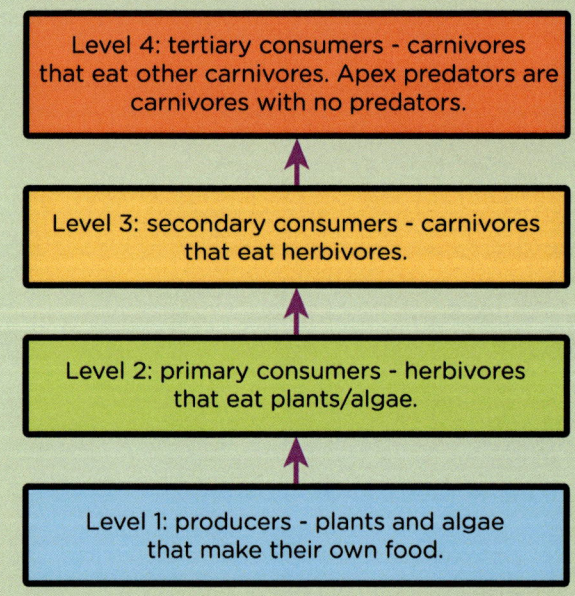

Food supply and biotechnology

Factors affecting food security
All specs except: CCEA

- Food security means having **sufficient, safe, and nutritious** food available to **meet the dietary needs of a population.** It depends on factors such as **availability, accessibility, and affordability** of food.
- Biological factors that are threatening food security include:
  - The increasing birth rate in some countries.
  - Changing diets in developed countries means scarce food resources are transported around the world.
  - New pests and pathogens that affect farming.
  - Environmental changes that affect food production, such as widespread famine occurring in some countries if rains fail.
  - The cost of agricultural inputs.
  - Conflicts can disrupt food production or destroy food and water infrastructure.
- Sustainable methods must be found to feed all people on Earth. This means:
  - **Sustainable:** preserving resources for future generations.
  - **Environmentally friendly:** reducing pollution and land degradation.
  - **Economically viable:** affordable for producers and consumers.
- Strategies include improving crop yields through biotechnology and better farming techniques, reducing waste in food production and supply chains, educating populations on nutrition and sustainable diets, and supporting smallholder farmers and ensuring fair trade.

Farming techniques
All specs except: OCR A, OCR B, CCEA, CIE

- The efficiency of food production can be improved by restricting energy transfer from food animals to the environment.
- This can be done through intensive farming to maximise yields by reducing energy use and biomass loss:
  - Limiting movement by having animals packed together in small pens.
  - Controlling the temperature of their surroundings.
  - Some people have ethical objections to some intensive farming methods, for example restricting movement may affect an animal's quality of life.
- Some animals are fed high-protein foods to increase growth.
- Crop rotation can be done, which may provide less encouragement for pests and be less damaging to soil.

Sustainable fisheries
Only: AQA, Edexcel, CIE

- Fish stocks in the oceans are declining.
- It is important to maintain fish stocks at a level where breeding continues, or certain species may disappear in some areas.
- Introducing fishing quotas and regulating net sizes play important roles in the conservation of fish stocks at a sustainable level.
- Preventing overfishing promotes the recovery of fish stocks.

Biotechnology

- The global human population is increasing rapidly, creating pressure on food supplies, land use, and healthcare.
  Modern biotechnology offers potential solutions through genetic modification (GM), microorganism culturing, and improved farming techniques.
- **Culturing microorganisms:**
  - Used to produce large quantities of protein-rich food efficiently.
  - Microorganisms are cultured in controlled conditions (industrial fermenters).
  - Benefits include fast growth, use of waste materials as feed, and small ecological footprint.
- **Fusarium and mycoprotein:**
  - Fusarium is a type of fungus used to produce mycoprotein – a meat substitute high in protein and fibre, low in fat.
  - Grown on a nutrient medium containing glucose syrup as an energy source
  - Aerobic conditions are maintained to support respiration.
  - The fungal biomass is harvested, purified, and processed into food (e.g. Quorn).
- **GM bacteria for human insulin:**
  - Initially, purified pig insulin was used, but this was less effective and some people had allergic reactions to it.
  - Now, biotechnology has enabled genes for human insulin to be inserted into bacterial DNA (usually *E. coli*) which are then cultured in fermenters to produce insulin as they grow. The insulin is harvested, purified, and used to treat diabetes.
- **GM crops:**
  - Crops that have had genes inserted to improve yield, resistance to pests/diseases, or nutritional value (e.g. insect-resistant maize, drought-tolerant wheat).
  - This helps increase food production in regions with poor soil or harsh climates.
  - For example, **golden rice** is genetically modified to produce beta-carotene, which the body converts to vitamin A – helps prevent vitamin A deficiency in developing countries.

Advantages of GM biotechnology	Concerns and considerations
Increased food production without needing more land	Safety concerns over potential long-term effects on the environment
Can improve the nutritional content of food (e.g. vitamins, amino acids) and help address malnutrition and starvation	May worsen economic disparities in poorer countries (e.g. dependence on biotech companies for seeds)
Can reduce the use of chemical pesticides and fertilisers	Biodiversity risks (GM crops may reduce variety in agriculture)
Can help address global health issues (e.g. insulin shortages, famines)	Ethical concerns over genetic modification interfering with nature

Science skills: Experimental procedures

Scientific processes
- Scientific ideas are not accepted until there is evidence to back them up.
  - Theories, theorems and experimental results are published in scientific journals. These undergo peer review by the scientific community before they are accepted.
  - Scientists will also repeat experiments described in journals to confirm their results are valid.
  - Some scientific ideas considered correct today were not initially accepted until decades after they were first published, such as Darwin's theory of evolution.
- Currently accepted scientific theories and models are the ones that best fit the current evidence and knowledge of the universe. They may be disproven in future.
- Scientific ideas that are reported in popular media before verification and peer review can lead to negative opinions of science.

Apparatus and equipment

Apparatus	Symbol
Bunsen burner: provides a constant flow of heat to a substance	↑ Heat
Beaker: stores water or other fluids. Other containers like canonical flasks may also be used depending on the experiment.	U
Test tube: holds a small amount of liquid. Larger tubes for heating are called boiling tubes.	U
Tripod: a stand that a Bunsen burner can be placed under. Gauze can be used to place a beaker on top.	A
Clamp stand: can be used in conjunction with clamps and bosses to suspend test tubes and other equipment in the air.	L
Funnel: directs liquid into a test tube or another container.	Y

- Various equipment can be used to take measurements during experiments. More precise equipment will lead to better results.
- Choosing the correct equipment and calibrating regularly can help ensure reliable results and reduce random errors.

Equipment	Used to measure
Ruler	Length
Measuring cylinder	Volume
Stopwatch	Time
Thermometer	Temperature
Pan balance/scale	Mass

Variables
- Scientific experiments are performed to determine the relationship between two or more variables.
- An **independent variable** is a variable that is manually changed. An experiment should have only one independent variable.
- A **dependent variable** is a variable that will change as a result of a change in the independent variable.
- The dependent and independent variables are measured to determine the relationship between them.
- A **control variable** is a variable that must be kept the same throughout the experiment to make the test fair.
- Changing a control variable will make it unclear if that change or a change in the independent variable is responsible for a change in the dependent variable.

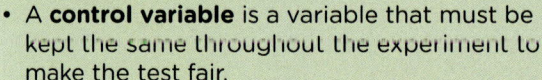
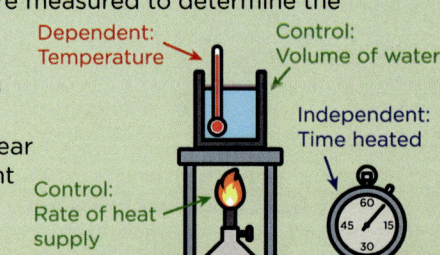

Safe experiments
- Measures should be taken so experiments are conducted safely.
- Sensible protective clothing should be worn, including **goggles** or safety visors to protect the eyes from harmful substances, **lab coats** to protect clothing from damage or harmful substances, and **gloves** when handling hazardous materials. Long hair should also be tied back so it is not a hazard.
- Steps should be taken to ensure **Bunsen burners** are used safely: using a heatproof mat underneath, and using **tongs** for any substances/equipment that is heated. The burner should be left on a yellow flame and gas taps should be turned off when not in use.
- Hazardous substances, such as chemicals or radioactive materials, should be handled with care and stored when not in use.
  - Containers should be correctly marked with their hazards (e.g. skin irritant).
  - Particularly dangerous substances should not be handled directly.
  - Flammable substances should be kept away from naked flames (e.g. ethanol).
- Biohazards, such as bacterial cultures, should be handled with care.
  - Aseptic techniques should be used when preparing bacterial cultures.
  - Disinfectant should be used after exposure to biohazards to prevent contamination.
  - Avoid contact with skin of stains (e.g. Toluidine blue or DCPIP)
  - Hands should be washed after handling biohazards or unsterilised samples.
- All equipment should be checked regularly.
  - Clamps and bosses should be tightly secured.
  - Electrical equipment should be inspected to ensure they have no live wires.

Science skills: Presenting and using data

Presenting data

- **Frequency tables** are used to record results from experiments. The first column should be the independent variable, and headers should include units

Example frequency table

Independent variable, x (s)	Measured variable, y (m)				Calculated dependent variable, y^2 (m²)
	1	2	3	Mean	
1	1.2	1.4	1.3	1.3	1.7
2	2.8	2.6	3	2.8	7.8
3	3.7	3.2	3.8	3.6	12.7

- **Bar charts** are used to compare categoric variables to continuous variables.
- **Histograms** show how a set of continuous data fits into grouped categories.
  - The height of each bar represents the frequency density.
  - The area of each bar is proportional to the number of data values in the group.
  - The bars should all be touching.
- **Line graphs** compare two continuous variables.
  - Recorded data is plotted onto a graph. The x and y coordinates of each point correspond to a value for the independent and dependent variable, respectively.
  - A smooth curve is drawn to show the general relationship. This should be close to as many points as possible, excluding outliers.

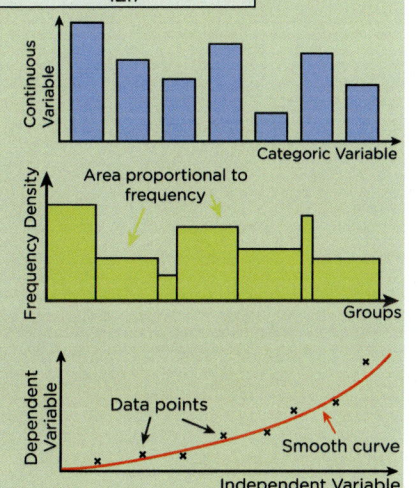

Rounding and standard form

- To round a value to a certain number of significant figures: identify the first non-zero digit in the value and count the number of digits after this. You will round this last digit up or down depending on if the next digit is greater than or equal to 5. Remove all digits outside the count (e.g. 0.005486 ≈ 0.0589 to 3 sig figs).
- Calculated values should be given to a number of significant figures equal to the lowest number of significant figures from the numbers used (e.g. the answer to 583 × 3.4 should be given to 2 sig figs.
- Values are rounded to the point where they should be the same as the true value rounded to that many significant figures.
- Standard form is used to write out very large or very small rounded numbers.
  - Write a number between 1 and 10 and multiply it by a power of 10. This can be positive or negative depending on if the number is big or small. Each multiplication by 10 moves the decimal point one digit to the left or right.
  - E.g. 158000 = 1.58 ×10⁵ and 0.00158 = 1.58 ×10⁻³.

Equations

- Equations show the relationship between scientific variables under certain conditions. To use an equation to find an unknown value using an equation:
  - Rearrange equation algebraically to make the unknown variable the subject.
  - Substitute in the values in the correct places, ensuring the units are the ones needed for the equation, and calculate the unknown value.
- Formula triangles can be used to help understand how to rearrange equations.
  - Cover the part of the triangle for the unknown value.
  - Divide the top value by the bottom value, or multiply the bottom values.

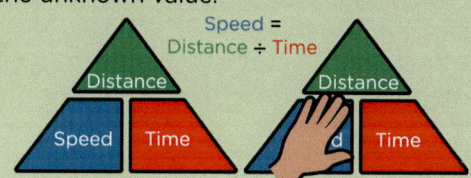

Interpreting graphs

- The **gradient** of a straight line of best fit can give information about the relationship between two variables in a graph.
- To calculate the gradient, choose two points on the lines as far apart as possible such that their x and y values are easy to read and calculate the differences in the two x and the two y values. The gradient will be **difference in y ÷ difference in x**.
- A curved **line of best fit** has a changing gradient. The gradient at a particular point can be calculated by drawing a tangent.
  - A **tangent** is a straight line that only just brushes against the point on the curve.
  - The gradient of the curve is the gradient of this straight-line tangent.
- The x or y intercept is the point where the line crosses the x or y axis.
- The **area under a line graph** is the value that corresponds to multiplying together the two variables shown in the graph as they are both changing.
  - For straight line graphs, this area can be calculated using the formula for the area of a rectangle or a triangle.
  - For curves, this area can be estimated by counting the squares beneath the graph.

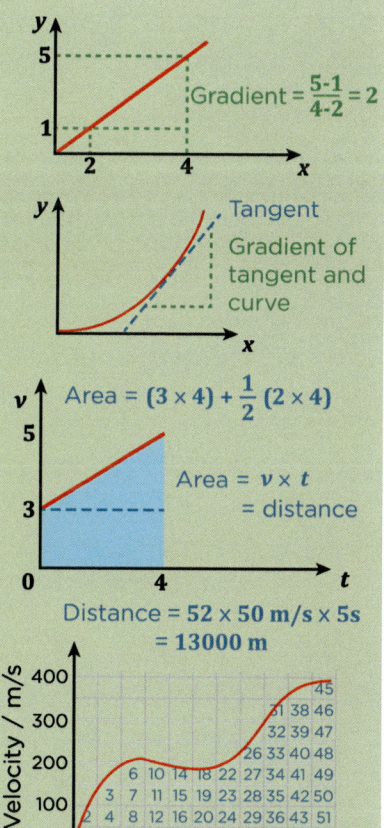

Science skills: Measuring results

Accuracy and precision

- The **true value** of a measurement is the value that would be obtained in an experiment without errors.
- The **accuracy** of a measurement is how close it is to the true value.
- The **precision** of a repeated experiment is how close together the measurements are.
- Accuracy and precision are two separate concepts. An accurate measurement is not necessarily precise and vice versa.

Accurate, not precise | Accurate and precise | Precise, not accurate

- A measurement is **repeatable** if the results are similar when the experiment is performed again by the same investigator, under the same conditions. This implies the measurements are precise.
- A measurement is **reproducible** if the results are similar when the experiment is performed again by a different investigator with different equipment. This implies the measurements are accurate.

Uncertainty

- The **uncertainty** of a measurement is the range of values for which it suggests the true value could lie within. Uncertainties are usually given as how far above or below a measured value the true value could be. For example, the value 37.4 ± 2 indicates the true value could be anywhere between 35.4 and 39.4.
- The uncertainty for a repeated experiment can be measured by the range of measurements about the mean. For example, the uncertainty of the measurements 3, 4, and 5 is 4 ± 1.

Length measured as 7 ± 3 cm

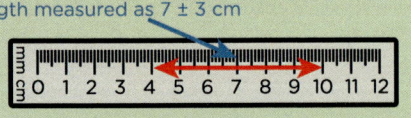

True length could be anywhere in this range

Errors and anomalies

- **Errors** will cause data to differ from the true value.
  - **Random errors** or anomalies affect single experiments and vary unpredictably, reducing the precision of the experiment.
  - **Systematic errors** involve measurement results differing from the true value by a consistent amount each time. This will reduce accuracy.
- **Anomalies** should be identified and omitted from the results. This can be done by:
  - Repeating experiments to find values that do not match others. For example, in the measurements 3, 7, 25, and 8, taken under the same conditions, the value 25 would be an anomaly.
  - Plotting results and seeing which values would not fit the pattern established by the rest of the data.

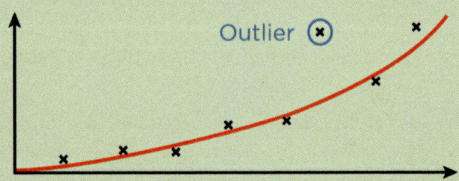

- **Systematic errors** can be prevented through careful planning of experiments. This includes:
  - Ensuring all control variables remain unchanged during the experiment.
  - Calibrating all equipment and using it correctly.
  - Turning off equipment between measurements to prevent heating if temperature is a variable.
  - Testing equipment before an experiment.
  - Only measuring the meniscus at eye level when using a measuring cylinder.

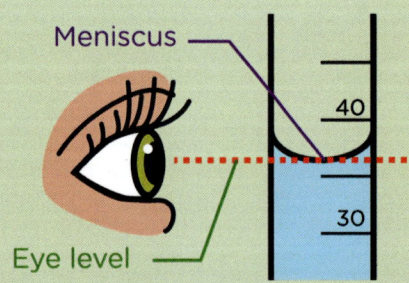

Mean and range

- The **mean** of a set of values is the sum of those values divided by the number of values there are (e.g. the mean of 4, 7, 13 is (4+7+13)/3 = 8). This is used to calculate the average value of the results from a repeated experiment.
- The **range** of data is the difference between the largest and smallest value (e.g. the range of 4, 7, 13 is 13 − 4 = 9). This can give us information about the uncertainty of a repeated experiment.

Units and prefixes

Unit	Symbol	Used to measure
Metre	m	Distance
Second	s	Time
Degrees Celsius	°C	Temperature
Litre	L	Volume
Grams	g	Mass
Joules	J	Energy
Coulombs	C	Charge

- Some units are derived as combinations of other units. For example:
  - Speed in metres per second, **m/s**.
  - Area in metres squared, **m²**.
  - Rate in grams per second, **g/s**.
  - Density in kilograms per meter cubed, **kg/m³**.
- Prefixes are added to units to indicate that they should be multiplied by a power of 10 to convert to the standard unit (e.g. 1 cm = 1 × 10^{-2} m). This makes them useful for very large or small values.
- When substituting values into equations, their units must be converted to have the correct prefix first.

Unit	Symbol	Multiplier
tera-	T	10^{12}
giga-	G	10^{9}
mega-	M	10^{6}
kilo-	k	10^{3}
centi-	c	10^{-2}
milli-	m	10^{-3}
micro-	μ	10^{-6}
nano-	n	10^{-9}